THE CRISIS OF PSYCHOANALYSIS

by Erich Fromm

A FAWCETT PREMIER BOOK

Fawcett Publications, Inc., Greenwich, Conn.

THE CRISIS OF PSYCHOANALYSIS

THIS BOOK CONTAINS THE COMPLETE TEXT OF THE ORIGINAL HARDCOVER EDITION.

A Fawcett Premier Book reprinted by arrangement with Holt, Rinehart and Winston, Inc.

Library of Congress Catalog Card Number: 70-102142

Printed in the United States of America
August 1971

THE CRISIS OF
PSYCHOANALYSIS

CONTENTS

PREFACE

THIS COLLECTION of essays, written at different times between 1932 and 1969, is unified by the common theme of the interrelation between psychological and sociological factors. The decision to publish the early papers, originally published in German, was made because they are still the most complete and adequate presentation of the theoretical basis upon which my later work on the subject rests. It seems to me they are particularly timely today, when there is a great deal of discussion on this topic, particularly on the relation between the theories of Marx and Freud, a discussion which, I am afraid, is sometimes amateurish and confusing. There is little I would change in these early papers, except that today I would not write them in terms of Freud's libido theory; but this hardly matters as far as the main trend of thought is concerned. I have resisted the temptation to make any changes in the substance of the papers, but have indicated discrepancies between what they present and my present viewpoint in footnotes; the only changes I made were to shorten essays where they seemed too lengthy or where they dealt with small points that are of little interest today.

The long opening essay, "The Crisis of Psychoanalysis," was written especially for this volume (along with the essay "The Significance of the Theory of Mother Right for Today," and the Epilogue). Dealing primarily with psycho-analytic theory and therapy, it attempts to analyze the social determinants of the development of psychoanalysis, as does the second paper with regard to Freud's Model of Man.

The chapters differ amongst themselves also, inasmuch as they were written for different occasions. For this reason they vary not only in style, but there is also a certain amount of overlapping. This could have been avoided only by cutting them, which would have destroyed the individual character of each paper. I hope the reader will bear with this, especially since, at times, even the overlapping statements are not identical but express the ideas on one point more fully than on another, so that they may even serve to clarify one another.

The essay on "The Crisis of Psychoanalysis" sums up a number of ideas that I developed more extensively in a larger, as yet unpublished, study under the tentative title *Humanist Psychoanalysis*, supported in part by Research Grant 5 ROIMH 13144-02 from the National Institute of Mental Health, U.S. Public Health Service.

I wish to express my warm thanks to Mr. Joseph Cunneen of Holt, Rinehart and Winston, who has been most helpful and understanding in editing this manuscript; to Dr. Jerome Brams for his assistance in the discussion of ego-psychology.

January, 1970

E. F.

1

THE CRISIS OF
PSYCHOANALYSIS

CONTEMPORARY PSYCHOANALYSIS IS passing through a crisis which superficially manifests itself in a certain decrease in the number of students applying for training in psychoanalytic institutes, and also in the number of patients who seek help from the psychoanalyst. Competing therapies have emerged in recent years which claim to have better therapeutic results and to require much less time and hence, of course, much less money. The psychoanalyst, who ten years ago was considered by the urban middle class to have the answer to its mental anguish, is now put on the defensive by his psychotherapeutic competitors and is losing his therapeutic monopoly.

In order to appreciate this crisis it is useful to consider the history of psychoanalytic therapy. Over half a century ago psychoanalysis opened up a new field and, economically speaking, a new market. Until then one had to be insane—or to suffer from painful and socially handicapping symptoms—in order to qualify for the psychiatrist's help. Less extreme psychic troubles were supposed to be within the province of the minister or the family doctor, and, in most cases, one was expected to handle them oneself and to suffer, if need be, silently.

When Freud started his therapeutic work he dealt with patients who were "sick" in the conventional sense of the word; they were suffering from aggravating symptoms like phobias, compulsions, and hysteria, even though they were not psychotic. Then analysis slowly began to extend its method to people who, traditionally, would not have been considered "sick." "Patients" came with complaints about their inability to enjoy life, about unhappy marriages, generalized anxiety, painful feelings of loneliness, difficulties in their capacity to work, etc. In contrast to past practice, these complaints were classified as "sickness" and a new type of "helper"—the psychoanalyst—was to take care of "difficulties in living," which until then had not been supposed to require professional help.

This development did not occur overnight but eventually it became a very important factor in the lives of the urban middle class, especially in the United States. Until not so long ago it was almost "normal" for a person of a certain urban subculture "to have his analyst"; a good deal of the time was spent on the "couch," just as people used to go to church or the temple.

The reasons for this boom of psychoanalysis are easy to recognize. This century, "the age of anxiety," has produced ever-increasing loneliness and isolation. The breakdown of religion, the seeming futility of politics, the emergence of the totally alienated "organization man," deprived the urban middle class of a frame of orientation and of a feeling of security in a meaningless world. Although a few seemed to find new frames of orientation in surrealism, radical politics, or Zen Buddhism, in general the disenchanted liberal was looking for a philosophy that he could subscribe to without any fundamental change in his outlook, i.e., without becoming "different" from his friends and colleagues.

Psychoanalysis offered the satisfaction of this need. Even when the symptom was not cured, it was a great relief to be able to talk to someone who listened patiently and more or less sympathetically. That the analyst was paid for his listening was only a minor drawback; maybe it was no drawback at all, because the very fact that one paid the analyst proved that this therapy was serious, respectable, and promising. Besides, its prestige was high because it was, economically, a luxury commodity.

The analyst offered a substitute for religion, politics, and philosophy. Freud had allegedly discovered all the secrets of life: the unconscious, the Oedipus complex, the repetition of childhood experience in the present; and once one understood these concepts, nothing remained mysterious or doubtful. One was a member of a somewhat esoteric sect, with the analyst as its priest, and one felt less puzzled as well as less lonely by marking time on the couch.

This holds true especially of those who were not suffering from circumscribed symptoms but from general malaise. The latter, in order to change in any meaningful way, would have had to have a vision of what a non-alienated person is like, of what it could mean to live a life centered around *being* rather than around *having* and *using*. Such a vision would have required a radical critique of their society, its overt and especially its hidden norms and principles; it would have required the courage to cut many comforting and protecting ties and to find oneself in a minority; it would have also required more psychoanalysts who in themselves are not caught in the psychological and spiritual mess of cybernated industrialized life.

One can often observe a "gentleman's agreement" between patient and analyst; neither of the two really wants to be shaken up by a fundamentally new experience; they are satisfied with small "improvements" and are unconsciously grateful to each other for not bringing into the open the unconscious "collusion" (to use R. D. Laing's term). As long as the patient comes, talks, and pays and the analyst listens and "interprets," the rules of the game are observed and the game is agreeable to both of them. Furthermore, the fact of having an analyst was frequently used to avoid a dreaded but unavoidable fact of life: that of having to make decisions and to take risks. When a difficult—or even tragic—decision could not be avoided, the addict to psychoanalysis transformed the real conflict into a "neurotic" one which needed to be "analyzed further," sometimes until the situation that required a decision had disappeared. All too many patients were no challenge to the analyst nor the analyst to them. Those who participated in the "gentlemen's agreement" unconsciously did not even want to be a challenge, since nothing should rock the boat of their "peaceful" existence. In addition, because psychoanalysts became increasingly sure of a large supply of patients, many of them tended to become lazy and to believe the marketplace assumption that their *"use value"* must be high because their *"market value"* was high. Backed by the powerful and prestigious International Psychoanalytic Association, many believed they possessed the "truth" after passing through the ritual from admission to graduation. In a world where bigness and the power of the organization are guarantees of truth, they were only following the general practice.

Does this description imply that psychoanalysis did not bring about any essential changes in people? That it was an aim in itself rather than a means to an end? By no means; it refers to the misuse of analytic therapy by some of its practitioners and patients, not to the serious work done successfully by others. Indeed, the facile denial of the therapeutic success of psychoanalysis says more about the difficulty of some fashionable authors to grasp the complex data with which psychoanalysis deals than about psychoanalysis itself. Criticism by people with little or no experience in this field cannot stand up against the testimony of analysts who have observed a considerable number of people relieved of troubles they complained about. Many patients have experienced a new sense of vitality and capacity for joy, and no other method than psychoanalysis could have produced these changes. Of course, others were not helped at all, and there were those in whom real yet moderate changes occurred, but this is not the place to analyze the therapeutic success of psychoanalysis statistically.

It is not surprising that many people were attracted by the promise that there are faster and cheaper methods of "cure." Psychoanalysis had opened up the possibility that one's misery could be alleviated through professional help. With the change in style to greater "efficiency," rapidity,[1] and "group activity" and with the spread of the need for "therapy" for people whose income did not suffice for prolonged daily sessions, the new therapies necessarily became very attractive and drew away a good many potential patients from psychoanalysis.[2]

Thus far I have only touched upon the more obvious

[1] Cf. Aniceto Aramoni, "New Analysis?" Paper read at the Third Forum of Psychoanalysis, Mexico, 1969. (To be published in *Revista de Psicoanálisis, Psiquiatría y Psicología,* Mexico.)

[2] The invention of group therapy, whatever its therapeutic merits (which I cannot properly judge due to lack of personal experience), did satisfy the need for a cheaper therapy and created a second basis for psychoanalytic therapy. And sensitivity groups are now a popular outlet for the need of making some kind of therapy part of mass culture.

and superficial reasons for the present crisis of psychoanalysis: the wrong use of psychoanalysis by a large number of practitioners and patients. To solve the crisis, at
least on this level, would only require making a stricter
selection of analysts and patients.

It is, however, necessary to ask: How could the misuse
occur? I have tried to give some very limited answers to
this question, but it can be answered fully only if we turn
from superficial manifestations to the deeper crisis in
which psychoanalysis finds itself.

What are the reasons for this deeper crisis?

I believe that the main reason lies in the change of
psychoanalysis from a radical to a conformist theory.
Psychoanalysis was originally a radical, penetrating, liberating theory. It slowly lost this character and stagnated,
failing to develop its theory in response to the changed
human situation after the First World War; instead it
retreated into conformism and the search for respectability.

The most creative and radical achievement of Freud's
theory was the founding of a "science of the irrational"—
i.e., the theory of the unconscious. As Freud himself
observed, this was a continuation of the work of Copernicus and Darwin (I would add also, of Marx): they had
attacked the illusions of man about this planet's place in
the cosmos and his own place in nature and in society;
Freud attacked the last fortress that had been left untouched—man's consciousness as the ultimate datum of
psychic experience. He showed that most of what we are
conscious of is not real and that most of what is real is
not in our consciousness. Philosophical idealism and traditional psychology were challenged head-on, and a further
step was taken into the knowledge of what is "really real."
(Theoretical physics took another decisive step in this
direction by attacking another certainty, that concerning
the nature of matter.)

Freud did not simply state the existence of unconscious
processes in general (others had done that before him),
but showed empirically how unconscious processes operate
by demonstrating their operation in concrete and observable phenomena: neurotic symptoms, dreams, and the
small acts of daily life.

The theory of the unconscious is one of the most decisive steps in our knowledge of man and in our capacity to distinguish appearance from reality in human behavior. As a consequence, it opened up a new dimension of honesty[3] and thereby created a new basis for critical thinking. Before Freud it was considered sufficient to know a man's conscious intentions in order to judge his sincerity. After Freud this was no longer enough; in fact, it was very little. Behind consciousness lurked the hidden reality, the unconscious, which was the key to man's *real* intentions. By analyzing a person (or using the analytic point of view in examining his behavior), the conventional view of bourgeois (or any other) "respectability," with its hypocrisy and dishonesty, was, in principle, shaken in its foundations. It was no longer enough for a man to justify his actions by his good intentions.[4] These good intentions, even if subjectively perfectly sincere, were subject to further scrutiny; the question was addressed to everyone: "What is behind it?" or better, *"Who are you behind yourself?"* In fact, Freud made it possible to approach the question "Who are you, and who am I?" in a spirit of new realism.

Freud's theoretical system, however, is beset by a deep dichotomy.[5] The Freud who opened the way to the understanding of "false consciousness" and human self-deception was a radical thinker (although not a revolutionary one) who transcended the limits of his society to a certain extent. He was to some degree a critic of society, especially in *The Future of an Illusion*. But he was also deeply rooted in the prejudices and philosophy of his historical period and class. The Freudian unconscious was mainly the seat of repressed sexuality, "honesty" referred

[3]It is generally believed that the sexual revolution was the result of Freud's theory. This seems to me questionable, especially because part of the new sexual freedom follows the consumption pattern of our present industrial society, as Aldous Huxley showed convincingly in *Brave New World*. However this may be, there is another and often neglected aspect of Freud's influence. One of the most significant elements in the protest of radical youth is precisely that against the sham and fraudulency of bourgeois society, expressed in its ideas as well as in many of its actions and in its language. Because he opened up a new dimension of honesty, Freud may be considered as one of the most important influences of youth's protest against sham.

[4]Marx's concept of "ideology" had the same meaning as Freud's "rationalization," although Marx did not try to examine the psychological mechanism of repression. (Cf. E. Fromm, *Beyond the Chains of Illusion*, The Credo Series, ed. Ruth Nanda Anshen, New York, Trident Press and Pocket Books, 1962.)

[5]Cf. the detailed analysis of this point in Chapter 2.

mainly to the vicissitudes of the libido in childhood, and his critique of society was restricted to its sexual repression. Freud was a bold and radical thinker in his great discoveries, but in their application he was impeded by an unquestioning belief that his society, although by no means satisfactory, was the ultimate form of human progress and could not be improved in any essential feature.

Because of this inherent contradiction within Freud and his theory, the question was: which of the two aspects would be developed by his disciples? Would they follow the Freud who continued the work of Copernicus, Darwin, and Marx, or would they be content with the Freud whose thought and feelings were restricted to the categories of bourgeois ideology and experience? Would they develop Freud's *special* theory of the unconscious, which was related to sexuality, into a *general* theory that would take as its object the whole range of repressed psychic experiences? Would they develop Freud's special form of sexual liberation into a general form of liberation through the widening of consciousness? To put it in another and more general way: would they develop Freud's most potent and revolutionary ideas, or would they emphasize those theories that could most easily be co-opted by the consumer society?

Freud could have been followed in both directions. However, his orthodox disciples followed the reformer, not the radical. They failed to develop the theory by liberating its basic findings from their time-bound narrowness into a wider and more radical framework. They were still trading on the aura of radicalism that psychoanalysis had before the First World War, when it was daring and revolutionary to expose sexual hypocrisy.

The ascendency of the conformist disciples was partly due to a particular trait in Freud's personality. He was not only a scientist and a therapist, but also a "reformer" who believed in his mission to found a movement for the rational and ethical reform of man.[6] He was a scientist, but despite his concern for theory, he never lost sight of

<hr>

[6]In 1910 still Freud toyed with the idea of suggesting to his adherents that they join the International Fraternity for Ethics and Culture, which should be transformed into the organization of the militant psychoanalysts. He soon dropped this plan in favor of the idea to found the International Psychoanalytic Association. Cf. E. Fromm, *Sigmund Freud's Mission*, World Perspectives, ed. Ruth Nanda Anshen, New York, Harper & Row, 1959, Chapter 8.

the "movement" and its politics. Most of those whom he made leaders of the movement were men without any capacity for radical criticism. Freud himself cannot have failed to know this, but he chose them because they had one outstanding quality: unquestionable loyalty to him and the movement; in fact, many of them possessed characteristics of bureaucrats of any political movement. Since the movement controlled both theory and therapeutic practice, such a choice of leaders was to have considerable influence on the development of psychoanalysis.

Other disciples defected: Jung, among other reasons[7] because he was a conservative romantic; and Adler, because he was a more superficial, though very gifted, rationalist. Rank developed original views, but was driven away, perhaps less by the dogmatic attitude of Freud than by the jealousy of his competitors. Ferenczi, perhaps the most lovable and imaginative of Freud's disciples, with neither the ambition to be a "leader" nor the courage to break with Freud, was nevertheless harshly rejected when he deviated in some important points toward the end of his life. Wilhelm Reich was removed from the organization although—or rather because—he had developed Freud's theory of sex to its ultimate consequences; he is a particularly interesting example of the fear of the psychoanalytic bureaucracy (and in this case also of Freud) to move from reform to a radical position in the very sphere that Freud had made the center of his system.

The victors in the fighting within Freud's court maintained a tight control, although there were many jealousies and rivalries among them. The most drastic manifestation of this inner fight among the members of the group is to be seen in Ernest Jones's "court biography," in which the author branded two of his chief rivals, Ferenczi and Rank, as having been insane at the time of their defection.[8]

Most orthodox psychoanalysts acknowledged the control of the analytic bureaucracy and conformed to its rules, or at least paid lip service to the required expression

[7]See Chapter 2.
[8]Cf. Michael Balint's letter to the editor of the *International Journal of Psycho-Analysis*, 34 (1958), 68. Cf. also my detailed discussion of Freud's attitude toward Ferenczi in *The Dogma of Christ* (New York: Holt, Rinehart and Winston, 1963), pp. 131-147. Also my discussion of Freud's attitude toward Ferenczi in *Sigmund Freud's Mission, op. cit.*, Chapter 6.

of loyalty. Nevertheless, there were also some who stayed within the organization and made important and original contributions to psychoanalytic theory and therapy, such as S. Rado, F. Alexander, Frieda Fromm-Reichman, the Balints, R. Spitz, E. Erikson, and a great many others. The vast majority of analysts within the organization, tended to see only what they expected (and were expected) to find. One of the most striking examples of this is that almost all orthodox psychoanalytic literature has ignored the obvious fact that the infant was intensely tied to his mother long before the development of the "Oedipus complex" and that this primary tie to mother is common to both boys and girls. A few of the more imaginative and bold psychoanalysts like Ferenczi, saw and mentioned this tie when describing their clinical observations, but when they wrote about theory they repeated Freud's formulations and did not make use of their own clinical observations.[9] Another example of the paralyzing effect of bureaucratic control is the unanimity with which almost all orthodox psychoanalysts accepted the theory that women were castrated men, in spite of the obvious clinical data as well as biological and anthropological considerations to the contrary. The same holds true in regard to the discussion of aggression. As long as Freud paid little attention to human aggressiveness, the writers within the psychoanalytic movement also neglected it, but after Freud's discovery of the death instinct, destructiveness became a central topic. Only in the acceptance of the concept of the death instinct did many balk (because, in my opinion, they were too tied to a mechanistic instinct theory to appreciate the depth of the new theory), but even they tried to conform by postulating a "destructive instinct" as opposed to the sexual instinct, thereby abandoning the old dichotomy between sexual and self-preservative instincts and at the same time keeping the old concept of instinct.[10]

[9]John Bowlby in his penetrating paper "The Nature of the Child's Tie to His Mother" has given a detailed history of psychoanalytic theory with regard to this point and has also called attention to the discrepancy between clinical description and theory among psychoanalytic authors (*The International Journal of Psycho-Analysis*, 34 [1958], 355-372).

[10]A most illustrative example for the degree to which adherence to the organization twisted even elementary human responses can be seen in the following letter from Michael Balint to the editor of the *International Journal of Psycho-Analysis* (*op. cit.*, p. 69):

Balint's letter reads:

"Sir,

"The publication of the third volume of Dr. Jones's great Freud

Biography created an awkward situation for me, Ferenczi's literary executor.

"In this volume Dr. Jones expresses rather strong views about Ferenczi's mental state, especially during the last years of his life, diagnosing it as a kind of slowly developing paranoia, with delusions and homicidal impulses in its final phase. Using his diagnosis as a basis, he interprets Ferenczi's scientific publications on the one hand, and his participation in the analytic movement on the other, in this sense.

"Undoubtedly Ferenczi's last period, which may be taken as having started with the *Genitaltheorie* (Thalassa) and the book written jointly with Rank, the *Entwicklungsziele* (Developmental Aims) is most controversial. It was during these years that Ferenczi advanced a number of new ideas which were felt at that time to be fantastic, revolutionary, exaggerated, without proper foundation, and so on. Moreover, on several occasions he himself had to withdraw or modify one or the other of the ideas just proposed, and it was also widely known that Freud adopted a rather critical attitude towards many—though far from all—of them.

"All this created a highly unfavourable aura which has made exceedingly difficult any proper re-evaluation of what was good and of lasting value among Ferenczi's ideas.

"If Dr. Jones's views about Ferenczi's mental state were now to remain unchallenged by me, who had made the whole Freud-Ferenczi correspondence available for the Biography, the impression might be created that I, Ferenczi's literary executor, one of his pupils and a close friend, were in agreement with them. This would certainly make the psychoanalytic public feel that the writings of the last period—when, according to Dr. Jones, his mental health was declining—do not merit proper attention. In my opinion exactly the opposite is the truth. Ferenczi's last writings not only anticipated the development of psychoanalytic technique and theory by fifteen to twenty-five years, but still contain many ideas that may shed light on problems of the present or even of the future.

"It is for this reason only that I wish to state that I saw Ferenczi frequently—once or twice almost every week—during his last illness, a pernicious anaemia which led to a rapidly progressing combined degeneration of the cord. He soon became ataxic, for the last few weeks had to stay in bed and for the last few days had to be fed: the immediate cause of his death was paralysis of the respiratory centre. Despite his progressive physical weakness, mentally he was always clear and on several occasions discussed with me in detail his controversy with Freud, his various plans how to re-write and enlarge his last Congress paper—if he were ever able to take a pen in his hand again. I saw him on the Sunday before his death; even then—though painfully weak and ataxic—mentally he was quite clear.

"True, as in every one of us, there were some neurotic traits in Ferenczi, among them a touchiness and an inordinate need to be loved and appreciated—correctly described by Dr. Jones. In addition, it is possible that Dr. Jones when arriving at his diagnosis had access to other sources than those he mentioned. Still, in my opinion the chief difference between Dr. Jones and myself is not so much in respect of facts as in respect of their interpretation which strongly suggests that it is caused, at any rate partly, by some subjective factor. Whether our difference has other sources or not, I would like to propose that for the time being we record our disagreement and entrust the next generation with the task of sorting out the truth.

Yours, etc., Michael Balint."

Dr. Ernest Jones comments:

"I certainly sympathize with Dr. Balint in his rather painful situation. Naturally it would not occur to me to doubt the faithfulness of his memory or the accuracy of his observations. He omitted to mention, however, that they are quite compatible with a more serious diagnosis, since it is a characteristic of paranoid patients to mislead friends and relatives by exhibiting complete lucidity on most topics.

"Nor should I expect Dr. Balint to doubt my own bona fides. What I wrote about Ferenczi's last days was based on the trustworthy evidence of an eye-witness.

The foregoing remarks may seem to imply that Freud bears all the blame for the sterility of orthodox psychoanalytic thought. But this would certainly be an unwarranted conclusion. After all, the analysts who submitted in this way were not forced by anyone to do so; they were free to think as they pleased. The worst that could have happened to them would have been expulsion from the organization, and, in fact, there were a few who took the "bold" step without any harmful effect, except that of being stigmatized by the bureaucracy as not being psychoanalysts. What was it that prevented this boldness?

One reason is obvious. Freud had developed a system that was attacked and ridiculed by almost all "respectable" professionals and academicians, because at that time it challenged many taboos and customary ideas. The individual analyst was made insecure by the hostility surrounding him, and it is understandable that he sought strength by belonging to an organization which assured him that he

---

"The varying value of Ferenczi's last writings remains, as Dr. Balint rightly remarks, controversial. I merely recorded my acquiescence in the opinions expressed so firmly by Freud, Eitingon, and everyone I knew in 1933 that they had been to some extent influenced by subjective personal factors.

Ernest Jones"

Balint's letter hardly needs any comment. Here is a very decent and intelligent man, a pupil and close friend of Ferenczi. He feels obliged to present the facts as he observed them and to correct Jones's statement about his teacher's alleged mental illness ("paranoid schizophrenia"). He points out that until the day of his death Ferenczi, who suffered from pernicious anaemia, was always mentally clear. This is an unequivocal statement which implies that Jones's statement was untrue. But how does Balint express his correction? He begins by saying that Ferenczi's writings in the last period were "most controversial" ("revolutionary" is joined to "fantastic," "exaggerated," and "without foundation"). Then he emphasizes that he is correcting Jones's statement *only* in his capacity as literary executor, in order to prevent the public from losing interest in Ferenczi's latest writings. He then follows his statement of the fact of Ferenczi's sanity by first speaking of Ferenczi's neurotic traits and makes the reservation that Jones may have "other sources" for his diagnosis which he did not mention. Finally, contradicting his own central statement, he ends up by saying that the next generation must be entrusted with finding the truth. This reference to other (unnamed) sources does not make much sense. If Balint, who is a psychiatrist, had no doubt about Ferenczi's sanity, how can one assume "another source" could have arrived at the opposite result, especially since Jones does not cite any evidence brought forward by this other source, which he could have done even without mentioning the name—if this other source existed, at least as a serious source of information.

If such a tortuous and submissive letter had been written by a lesser person than Balint, or if it had been written in a dictatorial system in order to avoid severe consequences for freedom or life, it would be understandable. But considering the fact that it was written by a well-known analyst living in England, it only shows the intensity of the pressure which forbids any but the mildest criticism of one of the leaders of the Organization.

was not alone, that he was a member of a fighting sect, and that by strict obedience to the organization he would be protected by it once he had been properly "ordained." It was also natural that together with the belief in the organization a certain "cult of personality" would develop.

Still another factor must be taken into consideration. Psychoanalysis claimed to have the answer to the riddle of the human mind. It had, indeed, some "answers"—if there were such a thing in this field—to one aspect of this riddle; however, considering the vastness of the problem, there was much more that was still not understood. If the individual analyst had been aware of the fragmentary character of his knowledge—both theoretically and therapeutically—he would have felt most insecure in a situation in which even that which he did know was rejected or ridiculed. Was it not natural, therefore, for him to support the fiction that, essentially, Freud had found the whole truth and that by magic participation he, as a member of the organization, shared in this possession of the truth? Of course, he could have accepted the fact of the fragmentary and tentative character of his knowledge, but this would have required not only a good deal of independence and courage but also productive thinking. It would have required every analyst to have the attitude of an inquiring man of research rather than that of a professional man simply trying to use his theory to make a living.

Obviously, the same process of bureaucratization and the alienation of thought, which I have described here with regard to the psychoanalytic movement, can be observed in the history of many political, philosophical, and religious movements. It is relatively rare in the history of science; otherwise, most creative scientific ideas would have been bogged down and their development stopped by the spirit of bureaucracy and dogmatism.[11] I have sketched this development in the psychoanalytic movement in some detail because it is a major, although insufficiently recognized, factor, in which the crisis of psychoanalysis is rooted.[12]

[11]The distortion of Marx's theoretical discoveries by Stalinism and the transitory destruction of the science of genetics by the Lysenko school under Stalin are good examples of bureaucratic distortions of science.

[12]It should be noted that in recent years the psychoanalytic bureaucracy has become a great deal more liberal than it used to be. The main reason for this liberalization probably lies in the fact that the contribution of its most original members deviates considerably from the norms for "right

In describing the negative effects of the bureaucratic nature of the psychoanalytic movement, we are dealing only with *one* factor contributing to the crisis of psychoanalysis. More important are the social changes that occurred with ever-increasing rapidity after the First World War. While bourgeois liberalism at the beginning of the century still had elements of radical critique and reform, the bulk of the middle class became more conservative as the stability of the system was threatened by new economic and political forces. Cybernation, the emergence of the "organization man" with the accompanying loss of individuality, dictatorships in important parts of the world, the threat of nuclear war,—these were some of the more important factors that put the middle class on the defensive. Most psychoanalysts, sharing the anxieties of the middle class, shared their defensiveness and cautiousness as well.

In contrast to this majority there was a small minority of radical psychoanalysts—the psychoanalytic "left"—who tried to continue and develop the system of the radical Freud, and to create a harmony between the psychoanalytic views of Freud and the sociological and psychological views of Marx. Among them are S. Bernfeld and Wilhelm Reich, who tried to achieve a synthesis between Freudianism and Marxism.[13] My own work also has dealt with the same problem, beginning with *Psychoanalyse und Soziologie* (1928) and *Das Christusdogma* (1930).[14] More recently R. D. Laing, one of the most

thinking" which were enforced up to some time ago. Had this liberalization not taken place, the movement would have been deprived of so many of its productive members that it could hardly have continued to exist. This liberalization was furthered by the threat arising from competing independent individual analysts, psychoanalytic societies, and training institutes. One symptomatic expression of this liberalization is the existence of two or more independent societies in various countries, differing in the degree of their adherence to Freudian dogma yet being member societies of the organization. Nevertheless, bureaucratic control has by no means disappeared, and for this reason many psychoanalysts have either left the London organization, were driven out, or have not been accepted by it. An "International Federation of Psychoanalytic Societies," which is not unified by a particular school of psychoanalytic theory and which has as its only aim scientific exchange among its member societies, has been formed in recent years.

[13] In later years, during his stay in the United States, Reich turned completely away from Marxist theory and lost all sympathy with socialism which he thought to be inferior to the liberal politics of Roosevelt and Eisenhower. (Cf. Ilse Reich-Ollendorf, *Wilhelm Reich*.) St. Martin's Press, Inc., New York, 1969.

[14] English translation in *The Dogma of Christ* (Holt, Rinehart & Winston, Inc., New York, 1963); these ideas were continued in the two papers of 1932 translated in the present volume as Chapters 8 and 9.

original and creative figures in contemporary psychoanalysis, has dealt brilliantly with the problems of psychoanalysis from a radical political and humanist position.

Not less important is the influence of psychoanalysis on the radical artistic and literary avant-garde. It is a very interesting phenomenon that the radical possibilities of Freud's theory, while largely neglected by the professional analysts, exercised a great attraction for radical movements in entirely different fields. This influence was particularly notable among the surrealists, although not restricted to them.

The last ten years have also shown an increasing preoccupation with the problem of psychoanalysis by a number of politically radical philosophers.[15] Jean-Paul Sartre has made some very interesting contributions to psychoanalytic thinking within the framework of his own existentialist philosophy. Apart from Sartre and Norman O. Brown, the best known among this group is Herbert Marcuse, who shares this interest in the connection between Marx and Freud with other members of the Frankfurt Institute for Social Research, such as Max Horkheimer and the late Theodor W. Adorno. There are also a number of others, especially Marxists and socialists, who in recent years have shown considerable interest in this problem and have written extensively about it. Unfortunately, this new literature often suffers from the fact that many of the writers are "philosophers of psychoanalysis" with insufficient knowledge of its clinical basis. One does not have to be a psychoanalyst in order to understand Freud's theories, but one must know their clinical basis; otherwise, it is all too easy to misunderstand Freudian concepts and to simply pick out a few vaguely appropriate quotations without sufficient knowledge of the whole system.

Marcuse, having written more extensively about psychoanalysis than any other philosopher, offers a good example of the particular distortion which the "philosophy of psychoanalysis" can inflict upon psychoanalytic theory. He claims that his work "moves exclusively in the field of theory, and keeps outside of the technical discipline which psychoanalysis has become." This is a bewildering state-

[15]The French journal *L'Homme et la Société* (Editions Authropos), for instance, published in 1969 a special issue on "Freudo-Marxisme et Sociologie de l'alienation."

ment. It implies that psychoanalysis started as a theoretical system and later became a "technical discipline"; the fact is, of course, that Freud's metapsychology was based on his clinical investigations.

What does Marcuse mean by "technical discipline"? Sometimes it sounds as if he is referring only to problems of therapy; but at other times the word "technical" is used to refer to clinical, empirical data. To make a separation between philosophy and analytic theory, on one hand, and psychoanalytic clinical data, on the other, is untenable in a science whose concepts and theories cannot be understood without reference to the clinical phenomena from which they were developed. To construct a "philosophy of psychoanalysis" which ignores its empirical basis must necessarily lead to serious errors in the understanding of the theory. Let me say again that I am not implying that one must be a psychoanalyst or even that one must have been psychoanalyzed in order to discuss problems of psychoanalysis. But in order to make sense of psychoanalytic concepts, a person must have some interest in and capacity to deal with empirical data, individual or social. Marcuse and others insist on handling concepts like *regression, narcissism, perversions,* etc., while remaining in the world of purely abstract speculation; they are "free" to make fantastic constructions precisely because they have no empirical knowledge against which to check their speculations. Unfortunately, many readers get their information about Freud in this distorted way, not to speak of the serious damage which all muddled thinking inflicts on those exposed to it.

This is not the place to enter into a full discussion of Marcuse's works dealing with psychoanalysis, *Eros and Civilization, One-dimensional Man,* and *An Essay on Liberation.*[16] I shall restrict myself to a few remarks. First of all, Marcuse, while widely read, makes elementary mistakes in presenting Freudian concepts. Thus, for instance, he misunderstands Freud's "reality principle" and the "pleasure principle" (although at one point he mentions the right quotation), assuming that there are several "real-

[16]Herbert Marcuse, *Eros and Civilization* (Boston: Beacon Press, 1955); *One-Dimensional Man* (Boston: Beacon Press, 1967); *An Essay on Liberation* (Boston: Beacon Press, 1968). In the *Essay* he has changed some of his former views and adopted others which he had sharply criticized, yet without indicating this explicitly.

ity principles" and asserting that Western civilization is governed by one of them, the "performance principle." Could it be that Marcuse shares the popular misconception that "pleasure principle" refers to the hedonistic norm that the aim of life is pleasure, and "reality principle" to the social norm that man's striving should be directed toward work and duty? Freud, of course, meant nothing of the kind; to him the reality principle was "a modification" of the pleasure principle, not its opponent. Freud's concept of the reality principle is that there is in every human being a capacity to observe reality and a tendency to protect oneself from the damage which the unchecked satisfaction of the instincts could inflict upon one. This reality principle is something quite different from the norms of a given social structure: one society may censor sexual strivings and fantasies very rigidly; hence the reality principle will tend to protect the person from self-damage by making him repress such fantasies. Another society may do quite the opposite, and hence the reality principle could have no reason to mobilize sexual repression. The "reality principle," in Freud's sense, is the same in both cases; what is different is the social structure and what I have called the *"social character"* in a given culture or class. (For example, a warrior society will produce a social character in which aggressive drives are fostered, while strivings for compassion and love are repressed; in a peaceful, cooperative society the opposite holds true. Or, in nineteenth-century Western middle-class society the strivings for pleasure and spending were repressed, while the anal-hoarding tendencies which result in the restriction of consumption and in pleasure in saving were encouraged; a hundred years later the social character is one that likes to spend and tends to repress the hoarding, stingy tendencies as inappropriate to the demands of society. In every society general human energy is transformed into specific energy which can be used by the society for its own proper functioning. Accordingly, what is repressed depends on the system of the social character, not on different "reality principles.") But the concept of character, in the dynamic sense in which Freud used it, does not appear in Marcuse's writings at all; one would assume that this is because it is not "philosophical" but empirical.

Not less serious is the distortion of Freud's theory in

Marcuse's use of the Freudian concept of repression. "'Repression' and 'repressive' in the non-technical sense," he writes, "are used to designate both conscious and unconscious, external and internal processes of restraint, constraint and repression."[17] But the central category of Freud's system is "repression" in the dynamic sense of the repressed being *unconscious*. By using "repression" for both conscious and unconscious data, the whole significance of Freud's concept of repression and unconscious is lost. Indeed, the word "repression" has two meanings: first, the conventional one, namely, to repress in the sense of oppress, or suppress; second, the psychological one used by Freud (although it had been used in the psychological sense before), namely, to remove something from awareness. The two meanings by themselves have nothing to do with each other. By using the concept of repression indiscriminately, Marcuse confuses the central issue of psychoanalysis. He plays on the double meaning of the word "repression," making it appear as if the two meanings were one, and in this process the meaning of repression in the psychoanalytic sense is lost—although a nice formula is found which unifies a political and a psychological category by the ambiguity of the word.

Another example of Marcuse's treatment of Freud's theories is the theoretical question of the conservative nature of Eros and the life instinct. Marcuse makes much of the "fact" that Freud attributes the same conservative nature (of returning to an earlier stage) to Eros as to the death instinct. He is apparently unaware that after some wavering Freud arrived, in the *Outline of Psychoanalysis*, at the opposite conclusion, namely that Eros does *not* partake of the conservative nature, a position Freud adopted in spite of the great theoretical difficulties it created.[18]

When stripped of much of its verbiage, *Eros and Civilization* presents as the ideal for the new man in the non-repressive society a reactivation of his pregenital sexuality, especially the sadistic and coprophilic tendencies. In fact, the ideal of Marcuse's "non-repressive society" seems to be an infantile paradise where all work is play and where there is no serious conflict or tragedy. (He never

[17]*Eros and Civilization, op. cit.*, p. 8.
[18]*Outline of Psychoanalysis*, Standard Edition, xx, p. 149.

comes to grips with the problem of the conflict between this ideal and the organization of automated industry.) This ideal of the regression to infantile libidinal organization is coupled with an attack against the domination of genital sexuality over the pregenital drives. By some juggling of words, the subordination of oral and anal erotic strivings under the primacy of genitality is identified with monogamous marriage, the bourgeois family, and the principle that genital sexual pleasure is permissible only if it serves procreation. In his attack against genital "domination" Marcuse ignores the obvious fact that genital sexuality is by no means bound to procreation; men and women have always enjoyed sexual pleasure without the intention to procreate, and methods to prevent conception date far back in history. Marcuse seems to imply that because the perversions—like sadism or coprophilia— cannot result in procreation, they are more "free" than genital sexuality. Marcuse's revolutionary rhetoric obscures the irrational and anti-revolutionary character of his attitude. Like some *avant garde* artists and writers from de Sade and Marinetti to the present, he is attracted by infantile regression, perversions and—as I see it—in a more hidden way by destruction and hate. To express the decay of a society in literature and art and to analyze it scientifically is valid enough, but it is the opposite of revolutionary if the artist or writer shares in, and glorifies the morbidity of a society he wants to change.

Closely related to this is Marcuse's glorification of Narcissus and Orpheus, while Prometheus (whom Marx, incidentally, called "the noblest saint and martyr in the philosophical calendar") is degraded to the "archetype hero of the performance principle."[19] The Orphic-Narcissistic images "are committed to the underworld and to death." Orpheus, according to the classical tradition, is "associated with the introduction of homosexuality." But, says Marcuse, "like Narcissus he rejects the normal Eros, not for an ascetic ideal, but for a fuller Eros. Like Narcissus he protests against the repressive order of procreative sexuality. This Orphic and Narcissistic Eros is the negation of this order—the Great Refusal."[20] This Great Refusal is also defined as "refusal to accept separation from the

[19]*Ibid.*, Chap. 8.
[20]*Ibid.*, p. 171.

libidinous object (or subject)"[21]; in the last analysis, it is
the refusal to grow up, to separate fully from mother and
soil, and to experience fully sexual pleasure (genital and
not anal or sadistic). (Oddly enough, in *One Dimensional
Man* the Great Refusal seems to have changed its meaning
completely though no mention of the change is made; the
new meaning is the refusal to use concepts which bridge
the gap between present and future.) That this ideal is
precisely the opposite of Freud's concept of human development and corresponds rather to his concept of neurosis and psychosis is well known.

This ideal of liberation from the supremacy of genital
sexuality, of course, is also the very opposite of the sexual
liberation which Reich proposed, and which is in full
swing today.

Marcuse ignores the fact that for Freud the evolution
of the libido from primary narcissism to the oral and anal,
and then to the genital level, is not primarily a matter of
increasing repression, but of the biological process of
maturing, which leads to the primacy of genital sexuality.
For Freud, the healthy person is the one who has reached
the genital level and who enjoys sexual intercourse;
Freud's whole evolutionary scheme is based upon this idea
of genitality as the highest stage of libido development. I
am not objecting here to Marcuse's deviation from Freud,
but to the confusion created, not only by using Freud's
concepts wrongly, but also by giving the impression that
he is representing Freud's position, with only minor revisions. In fact, he is constructing a theory that is the
opposite of all that is essential in Freud's thinking; this is
achieved by quoting sentences out of context, or statements made by Freud and later dropped, or by plain
ignorance of Freud's position and/or its meaning. Marcuse does more or less the same with Marx as he does
with Freud. While there is some slight criticism of Marx
for not having found the whole truth about the new man,
he gives the impression of standing, on the whole, for
Marx's aims for a socialist society. But he does not comment on the fact that his own ideal of the infantilistic new
man is exactly the opposite of Marx's ideal of a produc-

tive, self-active man, able to love and to be interested in everything around him. One cannot help feeling that Marcuse uses the popularity of Marx and Freud among the radical young generation to make his anti-Freudian and anti-Marxian concept of the New Man more attractive.

How is it possible that an erudite scholar like Marcuse can have such a distorted picture of psychoanalysis? It seems to me that the answer lies in the particular interest he—as well as some other intellectuals—have in psychoanalysis. For him psychoanalysis is not an empirical method for the uncovering of the unconscious strivings of a person, masked by rationalization, a theory *ad personam* which deals with the character and demonstrates the various unconscious motivations for apparently "reasonable acts." Psychoanalysis, for Marcuse, is a set of metapsychological speculations about death, the life instinct, infantile sexuality, etc. It was the great achievement of Freud to have taken up a number of problems so far only dealt with abstractly by philosophy and to transform them into the subject matter of empirical investigation. Marcuse seems to be undoing this achievement by retransforming Freud's empirical concepts into the subject matter of philosophical speculation—and a rather muddy speculation, at that.

Aside from the group of left analysts, and those inside the Freudian organization who were mentioned before, I want to mention here especially four psychoanalysts whose contributions are more systematic and have become more influential than most of the others. (I omit the early dissenters like Adler, Rank and Jung.)

Karen Horney was the first to take a critical approach to Freud's psychology of women, and later developed an approach which, dispensing with the libido theory and emphasizing the significance of cultural factors, arrived at many fertile insights.

Harry Stack Sullivan shared with her the recognition of the significance of cultural factors, and in his concept of psychoanalysis as a theory of "interpersonal relations" also rejected the libido theory. While his theory of man, in my opinion, is somewhat restricted by the fact that his model of man refers essentially to contemporary alienated man, his main achievement was his insight into the fantasy

world and communications processes of severely sick, and
especially schizophrenic patients.[22]

Erik H. Erikson has made significant contributions to the
theory of childhood, and the influence of society on childhood development; he has also furthered psychoanalytic
thought by his study of the problems of identity and by his
psychoanalytic biographies of Luther and Gandhi. As I see
it, he has not gone as far as he could have had he
followed in a more radical way the consequences of some
of his premises.

Melanie Klein and her school have the great merit of
having pointed to the deep irrationality in man by trying
to demonstrate its manifestations in the infant. While her
evidence and constructions have not been convincing in
the opinion of most psychoanalysts, including myself, her
theories had at least the function of an antidote against
the rationalistic tendencies that manifest themselves increasingly in the psychoanalytic movement.

The conformist tendencies among the majority of psychoanalysts found their main expression in that school
which I shall discuss in more detail because it has become
the most influential and prestigious in the psychoanalytic
movement: Ego Psychology. This school was started and
carried on by a group of psychoanalysts,[23] who in coop-
eration developed a system meant to complement the
classic theory while accepting what it had achieved thus
far.

The ego psychologists derive their name from the fact
that they have turned their theoretical attention to the *ego*
and away from what was the center of attention for
Freud's system, the *id*, the irrational passions which motivate man and yet are unconscious to him. This interest in
the ego has a respectable lineage. Especially since Freud's
division of id—ego—super-ego superseded the older dichotomy of the systems *ucs* (unconscious) and *cs* (con-

[22]Although Horney, Sullivan, and I are usually classified together as
a "culturalist" or "Neo-Freudian" school, this classification hardly seems
justified. In spite of the fact that we were friends, worked together, and
had certain views in common—particularly a critical attitude toward the
libido theory—the differences between us were greater than the simi-
larities, especially in the "cultural" viewpoint. Horney and Sullivan
thought of cultural patterns in the traditional anthropological sense,
while my approach was based upon an analysis of the economic,
political, and psychological forces that form the basis of society.
[23]The founders of the school are H. Hartmann, R. M. Loewenstein,
E. Kris. Among the other representatives of ego psychology are D. Rapaport, G. Klein, B. Gill, R. R. Holt, and R. W. White.

scious), the ego concept became a central concept in psychoanalytic theory. Freud's shift in terminology and to some extent in substance had, among other factors, been provoked by the discovery of unconscious aspects of the ego which seemed to make the older division somewhat obsolete. Anna Freud's *The Ego and the Mechanisms of Defense* (1964) formed another anchor for the claim that ego psychology was an organic development, the roots of which are to be found in classic Freudian theory.

The ego psychologists emphasized that Anna Freud's work was by no means a first statement of their position. It followed Freud's earlier investigations about the unconscious aspects of ego functioning. However, in spite of the correctness of quotations which establish Freud as the father of ego psychology, the claim to his paternity is not as valid as it seems to Hartmann and his group. While Freud showed increasingly greater interest in the ego, his analytic psychology remained centered around the unconscious drives that motivate behavior, and for this reason he was and always remained an "id psychologist."

Ego psychology makes its appearance with a paper written by its founder Heinz Hartmann and published in 1939, one year after Freud's death. In this paper, *Ego Psychology and the Problem of Adaptation*,[24] Hartmann laid the foundation for the new system by focusing on the process of adaptation. He makes the goal of his revision very clear. Psychoanalysis

started out with the study of pathology and phenomena which are on the border of normal psychology and psychopathology. At that time its work centered on the id and the instinctual drives. . . . At present we no longer doubt that psychoanalysis can claim to be a *general* psychology in the broadest sense of the word and our conception of the working methods which may properly be considered psy-

[24]First German publication, *Internationale Zeitschrift für Psychoanalyse und Imago*, 1939. English translation by D. Rapaport, New York, International Universities Press, 1958. Since the following presentation of ego psychology has necessarily to be brief, I shall deal here mainly with this paper, in which most of the important ideas of ego psychology are already indicated, without implying, however, that Hartmann and the other members of the school have not made significant additions and refinements in their later work.

I wish to acknowledge the assistance of Jerome Brams in a larger study I undertook on ego psychology.

choanalytic has become broader, deeper and more discriminating.[25]

This new concern of psychoanalysis as general psychology led the ego psychologist to concentrate his attention on phenomena which the older psychoanalysis had ignored and to which in later years it paid only marginal attention: that is, "those processes and working methods of the mental apparatus which lead to adapted achievements."[26] The thesis which has become the basis for the further development of ego psychology is that not every adaptation to the environment, every learning and maturation process, is a conflict; that the development of perception, intention, object comprehension, thinking language, recall phenomena, productivity, to the phases of motor development, grasping, crawling, walking, and to the maturation and learning processes occur outside of conflict. Hartmann next proposed the adoption of the provisional term *conflict-free ego sphere* for that ensemble of functions which at any given time exert their effects outside the regions of mental conflicts. Ego psychology stresses the role of the will and of the "desexualized" libidinous and "de-aggressived" destructive energy which provide the ego with the *energy* to exercise its functions, including willing.[27] While these concepts constitute a shift of emphasis away from Freud's concern with the irrational forces that determine the will and restrict the functioning of the ego, their treatment of the id and the ego constitutes an even more fundamental departure. Freud had looked at the id as an unstructured "cauldron of passions"; B. Gill proposes, with the approval of most ego psychologists, that the id itself has a structure, and if not logic, at least some prelogic. Ego and id are no longer viewed as opposites but as continua. It follows that the dichotomies assumed by Freud between pleasure and reality principle, mobile and bound energies, and primary and secondary processes are also presented as continua. They,

[25]*Op. cit.*, p. 4.
[26]*Ibid.*, p. 5.
[27]R. W. White has pointed out that ideas of "neutralization" and "deneutralization" of libido or aggressive energy are untenable in light of what is now known about the functioning of the nervous system. He proposes instead a concept of independent ego energies which are present from birth and which are used in the development and functioning of ego activities.

like the ego and the id, are conceived as a hierarchical continuum of forces and structures existing at all levels of the hierarchy. By this assumption of a continuum the dialectic element in Freud's concept has disappeared. Freud's main focus here as elsewhere was on the *conflict* between opposites and on the new phenomena produced by the conflict. This dialectic method of thinking yields to a view in which the concept of conflict between opposites is replaced by that of a developmental growth within a structured hierarchy.

The conformist character of ego psychology is shown more clearly in the ego-psychological reevaluation of Freud's principal goals than in these fine theoretical points. Freud expresses his goal for therapy and also for the development of man in the bold and poetic formulation, "Where there was id there shall be ego." This was the expression of Freud's faith in reason; it was the *raison d'être* for his method of liberating man by making the unconscious conscious. Hartmann, however, says Freud's statement has often been "misunderstood": "It does not mean that there ever has been, or could be, a man who is purely rational; it implies only a cultural-historical tendency, and a therapeutic goal."[28]

This is the positivistic version of a radical aim. The point that there never was, nor ever will be a *completely* rational man is a description of a tendency which becomes a truism by the qualifying word "completely." What mattered for Freud was not the *maximum* of ego development, but the *optimum* reachable by man. He established a *normative* principle based on his theory of man, namely that man *should* try to replace id by ego as far as he is able, because the more he succeeds in this endeavor the more he avoids neurotic and—what amounts to the same thing—existentially unnecessary suffering. Here is the precise difference between Freud, who postulates a *norm* for human development, and the positivist, who by referring to Freud's motto as merely indicating a "cultural-historical tendency" negates the radical *normative* essence of Freud's motto, which implies "should."

The same conformist tendency can be seen in Hartmann's statement about the concept of mental health. Hartmann criticizes those who "make hasty pronounce-

[28]Hartmann, *op. cit.*, p. 73.

ments about the attributes of 'ideal health' " and claims
that they "underestimate both the great variety of personality which must, practically speaking, be considered
healthy and the many personality types which are socially
necessary."[29]

What is meant by "practically speaking"? By the
vagueness of his language, Hartmann bypasses one of the
most significant problems in our field, that of the two
meanings of mental health. One meaning refers to the
functioning of the psychic system in terms of its optimal
growth; I call this a "humanist" concept because it is
centered around man. Freud's formulation that health
implies the capacity for love and work, is somewhat general, but it clearly implies that a person filled with hate
and destructiveness and incapable of loving is not healthy.
Or, to take something more specific, Freud would not
speak of a person who had more or less completely
regressed to the anal-sadistic level as "healthy." But could
such a person not function well in a particular kind of
society? Was not a sadist quite effective in the Nazi
system, and a loving person quite unadapted? Is the
alienated person with little love and little sense of identity
not better adapted to the technological society of today
than a sensitive, deeply feeling person? When speaking of
health in a sick society, one uses the concept of health in a
second, sociological meaning, as denoting adaptation to
society. The real problem here is precisely that of the
conflict between "health" in human terms and "health" in
social terms; a person may function well in a sick society
precisely because he is sick in human terms. The words
"practically speaking," therefore, imply that if a personality is desirable from the standpoint of society, the person is
judged healthy from a psychoanalytic viewpoint.

Hartmann has here removed the most important—and
radical element in Freud's system: the criticism of middle
class mores, and the protest against them in the name of
man and his development. With his identification of "human" and "social" health, and the implicit denial of social
pathology, he is in opposition to Freud who spoke of
"collective neuroses" and of the "pathology of civilized

communities."[30] Hartmann does not see that sexual repression in the Victorian middle class was in his sense "healthy" because the middle class had to develop a hoarding, anti-pleasure, and anti-spending social character as the psychological basis for that form of capital accumulation which was required by nineteenth-century economy. Freud spoke in the name of man, and criticized the customary degree of sexual repression as being conducive to mental illness.

In the middle of the twentieth century the problem is no longer that of sexual repression, since with the growth of a consumer society sex itself has become an article of consumption, and the trend in the direction of instant sexual gratification is part of the pattern of consumption that fits the economic needs of a cybernated society. In present-day society it is *other* impulses that are repressed; to be fully alive, to be free, and to love. Indeed, if people today were healthy in a human sense, they would be less rather than more capable of fulfilling their social role; they would, however, protest against a sick society, and demand such socio-economic changes as would reduce the dichotomy between health in a social and health in a human sense.

Ego psychology constitutes a drastic revision of Freud's system, a revision of its spirit, not—with some exceptions— its concepts. This kind of revision is the regular fate of radical, challenging theories and visions. The orthodoxy preserves the teachings in their original form, guards them against attack and criticism, but "reinterprets" them, adds new emphasis, or makes additions while claiming that they are all to be found in the words of the master. In this manner the revision changes the spirit of the original teaching while remaining "orthodox." The other type of revision, which I propose to call dialectic, revises the "classic" formulations, with the aim of preserving their spirit. Such a revision tries to preserve the essence of the original teaching by liberating it from time-conditioned, restricting theoretical assumptions; it tries to resolve contradictions within the classic theory in a dialectic fashion and to modify the theory in the process of applying it to new problems and experiences.

[30]Cf. Sigmund Freud: *Civilization and Its Discontents*, trans. J. Riviere, London, The Hogarth Press, 1935, pp. 141-142.

Perhaps the most important revision is what ego psychology has *not* done. It has not developed "id psychology"—that is, it has not tried to make contributions to that which is the core of Freud's system, the "science of the irrational." It has not contributed to the enlarging of our knowledge of unconscious processes, conflicts, resistance, rationalizations, transference. But even more important, ego psychology has also in its own field not used a critical, liberating analysis. The grave danger to the future of man is largely due to his incapacity to recognize the fictitious character of his "common sense." The majority remain fixed to outworn and unrealistic categories and contents of thinking; they consider their "common sense" to be reason. A radical ego psychology would analyze the phenomenon of common sense, the reasons for its strength and rigidity, the methods to change it. Briefly, it would make the critical examination of social consciousness one of its central concerns. But ego psychology has not concerned itself with these radical investigations; it has remained content with rather abstract and largely metapsychological speculations that do not enrich our knowledge, clinically or socio-psychologically.

Ego psychology put all the emphasis on the rational aspects of adaptation, learning, will, etc. (a traditional attitude which ignores the fact that contemporary man is suffering from the inability to will his future and that "learning" often makes him more rather than less blind). This is, of course, a very legitimate and important field of investigation, in which investigators like J. Piaget, L. S. Vysotsky, K. Bühler, and many others have made outstanding contributions, hardly matched by those of ego psychology. The latter have "elevated" psychoanalysis to the level of academic respectability by saying "we too" know that the libido is not all there is in the system man. In doing so they have corrected some of the exaggeration of psychoanalytic theory, but many of their ideas are new only for those who had believed that the libido theory can explain everything.

The ego psychological revision did not only start by studying the psychology of adaptation, it *is* in itself a psychology of the adaptation of psychoanalysis to twentieth-century social science and to the dominant spirit in

Western society. Seeking shelter in conformity is very understandable in an age of anxiety and mass conformity; however, it does not constitute progress in psychoanalytic theory, but retreat. In fact, it deprives psychoanalysis of the vitality that once made it such an influential factor in contemporary culture.

The question must arise why, if my analysis is correct, the leaders of the psychoanalytic movement did not exclude the ego psychologists from their ranks, as they did with other "revisionists." Instead, quite to the contrary, ego psychology became the leading school within the psychoanalytic movement, a fact that was symbolically expressed by the election of Heinz Hartmann as president of the International Psycho-analytical Association in 1951.

The answer to this question is twofold. On the one hand, the ego psychologists were eager to establish their legitimacy by emphasizing their proper credentials as "legitimate" Freudians. On the other hand, it seems that they satisfied the general longing of official psychoanalysis for adaptation and respectability. The knowledge and brilliance of the ego psychologists was apparently a great gift for a movement that had lost its "cause," had neglected the productive development of "id psychology," looked for theoretical recognition, and did not want to be disturbed in its uncritical pursuit of dated ideas and therapeutic practices. Ego psychology was the ideal answer to the crisis of psychoanalysis—ideal, that is, if one had abandoned the hope for a radical, productive revision that would have returned to psychoanalysis its original potency.

It is to be noted, however, that there are exceptions to this favorable acceptance of ego analysis by the orthodox majority. S. Nacht, one of the most outstanding among the orthodox analysts, has presented a critique of ego psychology very similar to the one I have just given. In a symposium on "The Mutual Influences in the Development of Ego and Id," Nacht writes: "The attempt to raise psychoanalysis toward the heights of general psychology . . . as Hartmann, Odier and de Saussure among others . . . would like to do, seems to me sterilizing and a regressive step, to say the least, if it is aimed at a change of our methodology."[31] While I differ from Nacht in many aspects, I share with him the conviction that the ego-psychological school constitutes a retreat from the essence of psychoanalysis.

In spite of some disquieting symptoms, however, psychoanalysis is far from dead. But its death can be predicted, *unless* it changes its direction. This is what is meant here by the "crisis of psychoanalysis." Like every other crisis, this too contains an alternative: slow decay or creative renewal. What the outcome will be cannot be predicted, but there are hopeful indications. It is becoming increasingly clear that the present crisis of mankind is a problem that requires for its understanding and solution a profound knowledge of human reactions and that psychoanalysis can make important contributions in this field. Besides, if one is really interested in research, psychoanalysis is a most challenging, exacting field, no less so than biology or physics, especially for those who combine the capacity for penetrating and critical thinking with the ability to observe subtle psychic processes in which one has to participate in order to be able to make observations.

To conclude, the creative renewal of psychoanalysis is possible only if it overcomes its positivistic conformism and becomes again a critical and challenging theory in the spirit of radical humanism. This revised psychoanalysis will continue to descend ever more deeply into the underworld of the unconscious, it will be critical of all social arrangements that warp and deform man, and it will be concerned with the processes that could lead to the adaptation of society to the needs of man, rather than man's adaptation to society. Specifically, it will examine the psychological phenomena which constitute the pathology of contemporary society: alienation, anxiety, loneliness, the fear of feeling deeply, lack of activeness, lack of joy. These symptoms have taken over the central role held by sexual repression in Freud's time, and psychoanalytic theory must be formulated in such a way that it can understand the unconscious aspects of these symptoms and the

[31]S. Nacht, "Discussion of 'The Mutual Influences in the Development of Ego and Id.'" Symposium held at the 17th Congress of the International Psycho-analytical Association in Amsterdam, Holland, on August 8, 1951. Reprinted in *The Psycho-analytic Study of the Child*, New York, International Universities Press, 1952, Vol. VII.

pathogenic condition in society and family which produce them.

Specifically, psychoanalysis will study the "pathology of normalcy," the chronic, low-grade schizophrenia which is generated in the cybernated, technological society of today and tomorrow.

2

FREUD'S MODEL OF MAN
AND ITS SOCIAL DETERMINANTS

To APPRECIATE THE social basis of Freud's views, it is useful to recognize from the outset that he was a liberal critic of bourgeois society, in the sense in which liberal reformers in general were critical. He saw that society imposes unnecessary hardships on man, which are conducive to worse results rather than the expected better ones. He saw that this unnecessary harshness, as it operated in the field of sexual morality, led to the formation of neuroses that, in many cases, could have been avoided by a more tolerant attitude. (Political and educational reform are parallel phenomena.) But Freud was never a radical critic of capitalistic society. He never questioned its socioeconomic bases, nor did he criticize its ideologies—with the exception of those concerning sexuality.

As for his concept of man, it is important to point out first that Freud, rooted in the philosophy of humanism and enlightenment, starts out with the assumption of the existence of *man* as such—a universal man, not only man as he manifests himself in various cultures, but someone about whose structure generally valid and empirical statements can be made. Freud, like Spinoza before him, constructed a "model of human nature" on the basis of which not only neuroses, but all fundamental aspects,

["Freud's Model of Man and Its Social Determinants" was read as a paper at the Third International Forum of Psychoanalysis held in Mexico, August, 1969.]

44

possibilities, and necessities of man, can be explained and understood.

What is this Freudian model?

Freud saw man as a closed system driven by two forces: the self-preservative and the sexual drives. The latter are rooted in chemophysiological processes moving in a phased pattern. The first phase increases tension and unpleasure; the second reduces the built-up tension and in so doing creates that which subjectively is felt as "pleasure." Man is primarily an isolated being, whose primary interest is the optimal satisfaction of both his ego and his libidinous interest. Freud's man is the physiologically driven and motivated *homme machine*. But, secondarily, man is also a social being, because he needs other people for the satisfaction of his libidinous drives as well as those of self-preservation. The child is in need of mother (and here, according to Freud, libidinous desires follow the path of the physiological needs); the adult needs a sexual partner. Feelings like tenderness or love are looked upon as phenomena that accompany, and result from, libidinous interests. Individuals need each other as means for the satisfaction of their physiologically rooted drives. Man is primarily unrelated to others, and is only secondarily forced—or seduced—into relationships with others.

Freud's *homo sexualis* is a variant of the classic *homo economicus*. It is the isolated, self-sufficient man who has to enter into relations with others in order that they may mutually fulfill their needs. *Homo economicus* has economic needs that find their mutual satisfaction in the exchange of goods on the commodity market. The needs of *homo sexualis* are physiological and libidinous, and normally are mutually satisfied by the relations between the sexes. In both variants the persons essentially remain strangers to each other, being related only by the common aim of drive satisfaction. This social determination of Freud's theory by the spirit of the market economy does not mean that the theory is wrong, except in its claim of describing the situation of *man as such*; as a description of interpersonal relations in bourgeois society, it is valid for the majority of people.

To this general statement a specific point must be added with regard to the social determinants of Freud's concept of drives. Freud was a student of von Brücke, a physiologist who was one of the most distinguished representatives of mechanistic materialism, especially in its German form. This type of materialism was based on the principle that all psychic phenomena have their roots in certain physiological processes and that they *can be sufficiently explained and understood* if one knows these roots.[1] Freud, in search of the roots of psychic disturbances, had to look for a physiological substrate for the drives; to find this in sexuality was an ideal solution, since it corresponded both to the requirements of mechanistic-materialistic thought and to certain clinical findings in patients of his time and social class. It remains, of course, uncertain whether those findings would have impressed Freud so deeply if he had not thought within the framework of his philosophy; but it can hardly be doubted that his philosophy was an important determinant of his theory of drives. This means that someone with a different philosophy will approach his findings with a certain skepticism. Such a skepticism refers not so much to a restricted form of Freud's theories, according to which in *some* neurotic disturbances sexual factors play a decisive role, but rather to the claim that *all* neuroses and all human behavior are determined by the conflict between the sexual and the self-preservative drives.

Freud's libido theory also mirrors his social situation in another sense. It is based on the concept of scarcity, assuming that all human strivings for lust result from the need to rid oneself from unpleasureful tensions, rather than that lust is a phenomenon of abundance aiming at a greater intensity and depth of human experiences. This principle of scarcity is characteristic of middle-class

[1] The dependence of Freud's theory formation on the thinking of his teachers has been described by Peter Ammacher (*Psychological Issues*, Seattle, University of Washington Press, 1962), and Robert R. Holt summarizes approvingly the main thesis of this work in the following: Many of the most puzzling and seemingly arbitrary turns of psychoanalytic theory, involving propositions that are false to the extent that they are testable at all, are either hidden biological assumptions or result directly from such assumptions, which Freud learned from his teachers in medical school. They became a basic part of his intellectual equipment, as unquestioned as the assumption of universal determinism, were probably not always recognized by him as biological, and thus were retained as necessary ingredients when he attempted to turn away from neurologizing to the construction of an abstract, psychological model. (Holt, "A Review of Some of Freud's Biological Assumptions and Their Influence on His Theories," in *Psychoanalysis and Current Biological Thought*, ed. Norman S. Greenfield and W. McLewis, Madison, University of Wisconsin Press, 1965.)

thought, recalling Malthus, Benjamin Franklin, or an average businessman of the nineteenth century. There are many ramifications of this principle of scarcity and the virtue of saving,[2] but essentially it means that the quantity of all commodities is necessarily limited, and hence that equal satisfaction for all is impossible because true abundance is impossible; in such a framework scarcity becomes a most important stimulus for human activity.

In spite of its social determinants, Freud's theory of drives remains a fundamental contribution to the model of man. Even if the libido theory as such is not correct, it is, let us say, a symbolic expression of a more general phenomenon: that human behavior is the product of forces which, although usually not conscious as such, motivate man, drive him, and lead him into conflicts. The relatively static nature of human behavior is deceptive. It exists only because the system of forces producing it remains the same, and it remains the same as long as the conditions which mold these forces do not change. But when these conditions, social or individual, change, the system of forces loses its stability and with it the apparently static behavior pattern.

With his dynamic concept of *character*, Freud raised the psychology of behavior from the level of description to that of science. At the same time Freud did for psychology what the great dramatists and novelists achieved in artistic form. He showed man as the hero of a drama who, even if he is only of average talent, is a hero because he fights passionately in the attempt to make some sense of the fact of having been born. Freud's drama par excellence, the Oedipus complex, may be a more harmless, bourgeois version of forces which are much more elementary than the father-mother-son triangle described by it; but Freud has given this triangle the dramatic quality of the myth.

This theory of drives dominated Freud's systematic thinking until 1920, when a new phase of his thinking began, which constituted an essential change in his concept of man. Instead of the opposition between ego and libidinous drives, the basic conflict now was between "life instincts" (Eros) and "death instincts." The life instincts, comprising both ego and sexual drives, were placed in

[2] This is discussed further in Chapter 9.

opposition to the death instincts, which were considered the root of human destructiveness, directed either toward the person himself or the world outside. These new basic drives are constructed entirely differently from the old ones. First of all, they are not located in any special zone of the organism, as the libido is in the erogenous zones. Furthermore, they do not follow the pattern of the "hydraulic" mechanism: increasing tension → unpleasure → detension → pleasure → new tension, etc., but they are inherent in all living substance and operate without any special stimulation; their motivating force, however, is not less strong than that of the hydraulically operating instincts. Eros also does not follow the conservative principle of return to an original state that Freud, at one point, had postulated for all instincts. Eros has the tendency to unite and to integrate; the death instinct has the opposite tendency, to disintegration and destruction. Both drives operate constantly within man, fight each other, and blend with each other, until finally the death instinct proves to be the stronger and has its ultimate triumph in the death of the individual.

This new concept of drives indicates essential changes in Freud's mode of thinking and we may assume that these changes are related to fundamental social changes.

The new concept of drives does not follow the model of materialistic-mechanistic thinking; it can, rather, be considered as a biological, vitalistic oriented concept, a change corresponding to a general trend in biological thought at that time. More important, however, is Freud's new appreciation of the role of human destructiveness. Not that he had omitted aggression in his first theoretical model. He had considered aggression to be an important factor, but it was subordinated to the libidinous drives or those for self-preservation. In the new theory destructiveness becomes the rival of, and eventually the victor over the libido and the ego drives. Man cannot help wanting to destroy, for the destructive tendency is rooted in his biological constitution. Although he can mitigate this tendency to a certain point, he can never deprive it of its strength. His alternatives are to direct his destructiveness either against himself or against the world outside, but he has no chance of liberating himself from this tragic dilemma.

There are good reasons for the hypothesis that Freud's new appreciation of destructiveness had its roots in the experience of the first World War. This war shook the foundations of the liberal optimism that had filled the first period of Freud's life. Until 1914 the members of the middle class had believed that the world was rapidly approaching a state of greater security, harmony and peace. The "darkness" of the middle ages seemed to lift from generation to generation; in a few more steps, so it seemed, the world—or at least Europe—would resemble the streets of a well-lighted, protected capital. In the bourgeois euphoria of the *belle époque* it was easily forgotten that this picture was not true for the majority of the workers and peasants of Europe, and even less so for the populations of Asia and Africa. The war of 1914 destroyed this illusion; not so much the beginning of the war, as its duration and the inhumanity of its practices. Freud, who during the war still believed in the justice and victory of the German cause, was hit at a deeper psychic level than the average, less sensitive person. He probably sensed that the optimistic hopes of enlightenment thought were illusions, and concluded that man, by nature, was destined to be destructive. Precisely because he was a reformer,[3] the war must have hit him all the more forcefully. Since he was no radical critic of society and no revolutionary, it was impossible for him to hope for essential social changes, and he was forced to look for the causes of the tragedy in the nature of man.[4]

Freud was, historically speaking, a figure of the frontier, of a period of a radical change of the social character. Inasmuch as he belonged to the nineteenth century, he was optimistic, a thinker of the enlightenment; inasmuch as he belonged to the twentieth century, he was a pessimistic, almost despairing representative of a society caught in rapid and unpredictable change. Perhaps this pessimism was reinforced by his grave, painful, and life-threatening illness, an illness which lasted until his death, and which he bore with the heroism of a genius; perhaps also by the disappointment over the defection of some of

---

[3] Cf. E. Fromm, *Sigmund Freud's Mission*, New York, Harper and Row, 1959.

[4] Freud expressed this new pessimism very succinctly in *Civilization and Its Discontents* (trans. J. Riviere, London, The Hogarth Press, 1935), where he portrays man as lazy and in need of strong leaders.

his most gifted disciples—Adler, Jung, and Rank; however this may be, he could never recover his lost optimism. But, on the other hand, he neither could nor probably wished to cut himself entirely loose from his previous thinking. This is perhaps the reason why he never resolved the contradiction between the old and the new concept of man; the old libido was subsumed under Eros; the old aggression under the death instinct; but it is painfully clear, that this was only theoretical patchwork.[5]

Freud's model of man also places great emphasis on the dialectic of rationality and irrationality in man. The originality and greatness of Freud's thought becomes particularly clear at this point. As a successor of the enlightenment thinkers Freud was a rationalist who believed in the power of reason and the strength of the human will. But Freud had already lost his rationalistic innocence, as it were, at the beginning of his work, and had recognized the strength of human irrationality and the weakness of human reason and will. He fully confronted himself with the opposition inherent in the *two* principles, and found, dialectically, a new synthesis. This synthesis of rationalistic enlightenment thinking and twentieth century skepticism was expressed in his concept of the unconscious. If all that is real were conscious, then indeed man would be a rational being; for his rational thought follows the laws of logic. But the overwhelming part of his inner experience is unconscious, and for this reason is not subject to the control of logic, of reason, and will. Human irrationality dominates in the unconscious; logic governs in the conscious. But, and this is decisive, the unconscious steers consciousness, and thus the behavior of man. With this concept of the determination of man by the unconscious, Freud, without being aware of it, repeated a thesis which Spinoza had already expressed. But while it was marginal in Spinoza's system, it was central to Freud.

Freud did not resolve the conflict in a static way, simply allowing one of the two sides to prevail. If he had declared reason the victor, he would have remained an enlightenment philosopher; if he had given the decisive role to irrationality, he would have become a conservative

[5]In *The Heart of Man* (New York, Harper and Row, 1964), I have tried to connect Freud's death instinct with the theory of anal libido. In a yet unpublished manuscript on *The Causes of Human Destructiveness*, I have analyzed the relation between sexuality and Eros in Freud's system.

romantic, as were so many significant thinkers of the nineteenth century. Although it is true that man is driven by irrational forces—the libido, and especially in its pregenital stages of evolution, his ego—his reason and his will are also not without strength. The power of reason expresses itself in the first place in the fact that man can understand his irrationality by the use of reason. In this way Freud founded the *science of human irrationality*—psychoanalytic theory. But he did not stop at theory. Because a person in the analytic process can make his own unconscious conscious, he can also liberate himself from the dominance of unconscious strivings; instead of repressing them, he can negate them, that is, he can lessen their strength, and control them with his will. This is possible, Freud thought, because the grown-up person has as an ally a stronger ego than the child once had. Freud's psychoanalytic therapy was based on the hope of overcoming, or at least restraining, the unconscious impulses which, working in the dark, had previously been outside of man's control. Historically speaking, one can look at Freud's theory as the fruitful synthesis of rationalism and romanticism; the creative power of this synthesis may be one of the reasons why Freud's thinking became a dominating influence in the twentieth century. This influence was not due to the fact that Freud found a new therapy for neuroses, and probably also not primarily because of his role as a defender of repressed sexuality. There is a great deal to say in favor of the assumption that the most important reason for his general influence on culture is in this synthesis, whose fruitfulness can be clearly seen in the two most important defections from Freud, that of Adler and of Jung. Both exploded the Freudian synthesis and reverted to the two original oppositions. Adler, rooted in the short-lived optimism of the rising lower middle classes, constructed a one-sided rationalistic-optimistic theory. He believed that the innate disabilities are the very conditions of strength and that with intellectual understanding of a situation, man can liberate himself and make the tragedy of life disappear.

Jung, on the other hand, was a romantic who saw the sources of all human strength in the unconscious. He recognized the wealth and depth of symbols and myths much more profoundly than Freud, whose views were restricted by his sexual theory. Their aims, however, were contradictory. Freud wanted to understand the unconscious in order to weaken and control it; Jung, in order to gain an increased vitality from it. Their interest in the unconscious united the two men for some time, without their being aware that they were moving in opposite directions. As they halted on their way in order to talk about the unconscious, they fell under the illusion that they were proceeding in the same direction.

Closely related with Freud's synthesis of rationality and irrationality is his treatment of the conflict between determinism and indeterminism of the will. Freud was a determinist; he believed that man is not free, because he is determined by the unconscious, the id, and the superego. *But*, and this "but" is of decisive importance for Freud, man is also not wholly determined. With the help of the analytic method he can gain control over the unconscious. With this position of alternativism,[6] which resembles in its essence that of Spinoza and Marx, Freud accomplished another fruitful synthesis of two opposite poles.

Did Freud recognize the moral factor as a fundamental part in his model of man? The answer to this question is in the negative. Man develops exclusively under the influence of his self-interest, which demands optimal satisfaction of his libidinal impulses, always on the condition that they do not endanger his interest in self-preservation ("reality principle"). The moral problem, which traditionally has been that of the conflict between altruism and egoism, virtually disappeared. Egoism is the only driving force, and the conflict is simply between the two forms of egoism, the libidinous and the material. It hardly needs to be demonstrated that in this view of man as basically egotistical, Freud is following the leading concepts of bourgeois thinking. Nevertheless, to say that Freud simply denied the existence of conscience as an effective element in his model of human nature would not be correct. Freud recognizes the power of conscience, but he "explains" conscience, and in doing so deprives it of all objective validity. His explanation is that conscience is the superego, which is a replica of all the commandments and prohibitions of the father (or the father's superego) with

[6]Cf. the discussion of alternativism in Fromm, *The Heart of Man, op. cit.*

whom the little boy identifies himself when, motivated by castration anxiety, he overcomes his Oedipal strivings. This explanation refers to both elements of conscience: the formal one—the *how* of conscience formation, and the substantial one, that is concerned with the contents of conscience. Since the essential part of fatherly norms and the fatherly superego is socially conditioned, or to put it more correctly, since the superego is nothing but the personal mode of social norms, Freud's explanation leads to a relativization of all moral norms. Each norm has its significance, not because of the validity of its contents, but on the basis of the psychological mechanism by which it is accepted. Good is what the internalized authority commands, and bad what it prohibits. Freud is undoubtedly right inasmuch as the norms believed in by most people as moral are, to a large extent, nothing but norms established by society for the sake of its own optimal functioning. From this standpoint his theory is an important critique of existing conventional morality, and his theory of the superego unveils its true character. But he probably did not intend to imply this critical aspect of the theory; it may not even have been conscious to him. He did not give his theory a critical turn, and he could hardly have done so, since he was not much concerned with the question of whether there are any norms whose contents transcend the structure of his society and correspond better to the demands of human nature and the laws of human growth.

One cannot talk about Freud's anthropology without discussing two special cases: that of man and woman, and that of the child.

For Freud only the male is really a full human being. Woman is a crippled, castrated man. She suffers from this fate, and can be happy only if she finally overcomes her "castration complex" by the acceptance of a child and husband. But she remains inferior also in other respects— for instance, she is more narcissistic and less directed by conscience than man. This strange theory, according to which one half of the human race is only a crippled edition of the other, followed Victorian ideas that woman's desires were almost entirely directed to the bearing and upbringing of children—and to serve the man. Freud gave clear expression to this when he wrote *"the libido is masculine."* Belief in this Victorian idea of woman as being without her own sexuality was an expression of the extreme patriarchal assumption of man's natural superiority over the woman.[7] The male, in patriarchal ideology, is more rational, realistic, and responsible than the female, and hence destined by nature to be her leader and guide. How completely Freud shared this point of view follows from his reaction to the demand for political and social equality of women expressed by J. S. Mill, a thinker whom Freud profoundly admired in all other respects. Here Mill is simply "crazy"; it is unthinkable for Freud to imagine that his beloved bride should compete with him on the market place, instead of allowing herself to be protected by him.

Freud's patriarchal bias had two further serious consequences for his theory. One was that he could not recognize the nature of erotic love, since it is based on the male-female polarity which is only possible if male and female are equals, though different. Thus his whole system is centered around sexual but not erotic love. Even in his later theory he applies Eros (the life instincts) only to the behavior of living organisms in general, but does not extend it to the male-female dimension even though, and in contradiction to this, he equated Eros and sexuality. The other equally serious consequence was that Freud completely overlooked for the largest part of his life the primary tie of the child (boy or girl) to the mother, the nature of motherly love, and the fear of mother. The tie to mother could be conceived only in terms of the Oedipus situation when the little boy is already a little man, for whom, as for father, mother is a sexual object and who is afraid only of the father, not the mother. Only in the last years of his life did Freud begin to see this primary tie,

[7]The full understanding of this patriarchal ideology would require a more detailed discussion. Suffice it to say here that women constitute a class dominated and exploited by men in all patriarchal societies; like all exploiting groups, the dominant males have to produce ideologies in order to explain their domination as being natural, and hence as necessary and justified. Women, like most dominated classes, have accepted the male ideology, although privately they often carried with them their own and opposite ideas. It seems that the liberation of women began in the twentieth century and it goes together with a weakening of the patriarchal system in industrial society, although complete equality of women, *de facto*, even today does not exist in any country. The basis for the analysis of patriarchal/matriarchal societies was laid by J. J. Bachofen in his main opus, *Das Mutterrecht*, 1859, and the whole problem can hardly be understood fully without a knowledge of Bachofen's work. A translation of his selected writings was published in 1967, *Myth, Religion and the Mother Right*, ed. by Joseph Campbell, Princeton, N.J., Princeton University Press. Cf. Ch. 6 and 7.

although by no means in all its importance.[8] It seems
that aside from the repression of his own strong fixation to
his mother, Freud's patriarchal bias did not permit him
consciously to consider the woman-mother as the powerful figure to which the child is bound.[9] Almost all other
analysts accepted Freud's theories of sexuality and the
secondary role of mother, in spite of the overwhelming
evidence to the contrary.

Here, as everywhere else, pointing to the connection
between the theory and its social determinants, of course,
does not prove that the theory is wrong; but if one
examines the clinical evidence carefully, it does not
confirm Freud's theory. I cannot discuss it in this context;
a number of psychoanalysts, especially Karen Horney's
pioneering work with regard to the point, have presented
clinical findings which contradict Freud's hypothesis.[10]
In general, it may simply be said that Freud's theory in
this field, while always imaginative and fascinating because
of its logic, seems to contain only a minimum of truth,
probably because Freud was so deeply imbued by his
patriarchal bias.

Freud's picture of the child is quite a different matter.
Like the woman, the child also has been the object of
oppression and exploitation by the father throughout history. It was, like slave and wife, the property of the
man-father, who had "given" it life, and who could do
with it whatever he liked, arbitrarily and unrestrictedly, as
with all property. (The institution of the sacrifice of children, which was once so widespread in the world, is one
of the many manifestations of this constellation.)

Children could defend themselves even less than women
and slaves. Women have fought a guerrilla war against the
patriarchate in their own way; slaves have rebelled many
times in one form or the other. But temper tantrums,
refusal to eat, constipation, and bed-wetting are not the
weapons by which one can overthrow a powerful system.
The only result was that the child developed into a crip-

[8]Cf. the excellent paper by John Bowlby, "The Nature of the Child's
Tie to His Mother," *The International Journal of Psycho-Analysis*, 34
(1958), 355-372.
[9]For the same reason Freud also ignored J. J. Bachofen's rich material
on Mother Right, although he briefly referred to it a few times.
[10]See also Ashley Montagu's writings on this problem.

pled, inhibited, and often evil adult, who took revenge on
his own children for what had been done to him.

The domination of children was expressed, if not in
brutal, physical terms, then in psychic exploitation. The
adult demanded from the child the satisfaction of his
vanity, of his wish for obedience, the adaptation to his
moods, etc. Of special importance is the fact that the
adult did not take the child seriously. The child, one
assumed, has no psychic life of its own; it was supposed to
be a blank sheet of paper on which the adult had the right
and the obligation to write the text (another version of
"the white man's burden"). It followed from this that one
believed it to be right to lie to children. If a man lies to
adults he has to excuse it in some way. Lying to the child
apparently did not require any excuses, because, after all,
the child is not a full human being. The same principle is
employed towards adults when they are strangers, enemies, sick, criminals, or members of an inferior and exploited class or race. By and large, only those who are not
powerless have the right to demand the truth—this is the
principle that has been applied in most societies in history,
even though this was not their conscious ideology.

The *revolution of the child*, like that of the woman,
began in the nineteenth century. People began to see that
the child was not a blank sheet of paper, but a very
developed, curious, imaginative, sensitive being, in need of
stimulation. One symptom of this new appreciation of the
child, in the field of education, was the Montessori method; another, the much more influential theory of Freud.
He expressed the view, and could prove it clinically, that
unfavorable influences in childhood have the most aggravating consequences for later development. He could describe the peculiar and complicated mental and emotional
processes in the child. He emphasized particularly the
fact, which was generally denied, that the child is a
passionate being, with sensuous drives and fantasies that
give his life a dramatic quality.

Freud went furthest in this radically new appreciation
of the child when he assumed in the beginning of his
clinical work that many neuroses have their origin in acts
of sexual seduction of children by adults—and particularly, by their parents. At this moment he became, so to
speak, the accuser against parental exploitation in the

name of the integrity and freedom of the child. However, if one considers the intensity of Freud's rootedness in the patriarchal authoritarian system, it is not surprising that he later abandoned this radical position. He found that his patients had projected their own infantile desires and fantasies on to the parents in a number of cases and that in reality no such seduction had taken place. He generalized these cases and came to the conclusion, in agreement with his libido theory, that the child was a little criminal and pervert who only in the course of the evolution of the libido matures into a "normal" human being. Thus Freud arrived at a picture of the "sinful child" which, as some observers have commented, resembles the Augustinian picture of the child in essential points.[11]

After this change, the slogan was, so to speak, "the child is guilty"; his drives lead him into conflicts and these conflicts, if poorly solved, result in neurotic illness. I cannot help suspecting that Freud was motivated in this change of opinion not so much by his clinical findings, but by his faith in the existing social order and its authorities. This suspicion is supported by several circumstances, first of all by the categorical fashion in which Freud declared that all memories of parental seduction are fantasies. Is such a categorical statement not in contrast to the fact that adult incestuous interest in their children is by no means rare?

Another reason for the assumption of Freud's partisanship in favor of parents lies in the treatment of parental figures, which is to be found in his published case histories. It is surprising to see how Freud falsifies the picture of parents and attributes qualities to them that are clearly in contrast to the facts he himself presents. As I have tried to show in the example of his case history of Little Hans, Freud mentions the lack of threats on the part of Hans' parents who are fully concerned with the welfare of the child, when in fact threats and seduction are so clearly present that one has to shut one's eyes in order not to see them. The same observation can be made in other case histories.

The interpretation of Freud's shift from being an advocate of the child to a defender of the parents is indirect-

[11]For instance Robert Wälder, one of the most learned and uncompromising representatives of Freudian orthodoxy.

ly supported by the testimony of S. Ferenczi, one of
Freud's most experienced and imaginative disciples. In his
last years, Ferenczi, who never wavered in his loyalty to
Freud, was caught in a severe conflict with the master.[12]
Ferenczi had developed ideas which deviated from those
of Freud in two important points, and Freud reacted with
such sharpness that he did not shake hands with Ferenczi
at the latter's last visit.[13] One "deviation," which interests us less in this context, was the insistence that the
patient needs, for his cure, not only interpretation, but
also the love of the analyst (love understood here in a
non-sexual, non-exclusive sense). A more important deviation for our present purpose was Ferenczi's thesis that
Freud had been right after all in his original view: that in
reality, adults were in many instances the seducers of
children and that it was not always a matter of fantasies,
rooted in the child.

Aside from the importance of Ferenczi's clinical observation, one has to raise the question why Freud reacted so
violently and passionately. Was it a matter of something
more important than a clinical problem? It is not too
far-fetched to suppose that the main point was not the
correctness of the clinical theory, but the attitude toward
authority. If it is true that Freud had withdrawn his
original radical critique of the parents—that is, of social
authority—and had adopted a position in favor of authority, then, indeed, one may suspect that his reaction was due
to his ambivalence to social authority, and that he reacted
violently when he was reminded of the position he had
given up, of, as it were, his "betrayal" of the child.

The conclusion of this sketch of Freud's picture of man
requires a word on his concept of history. Freud developed the nucleus of a philosophy of history, although
he did not intend to offer any systematic presentation. At
the beginning of history, we find man without culture,
completely dedicated to the satisfaction of his instinctual
drives, and happy to that extent. This picture, however, is
in contrast to another, which assumes a conflict even in
this first phase of complete instinctual satisfaction.

Man must leave this paradise precisely because the

---

[12]Cf. a detailed description of this conflict in Fromm's *Sigmund Freud's
Mission, op. cit.*
[13]Personal communication from the late Mrs. Izzette de Forest, one
of Ferenczi's students and friends.

unlimited satisfaction of his drives leads to the conflict of the sons with the father, to the murder of the father, and eventually to the formation of the incest taboo. The rebellious sons gain a battle, but they lose the war against the fathers, whose prerogatives are now secured forever by "morality" and the social order (here again we are reminded of Freud's ambivalence toward authority).

While in this aspect of Freud's thinking a state of unrestricted instinctual satisfaction was *impossible* in the long run, he develops another thesis which is quite different. The possibility of this paradisical state is not denied, but it is assumed that man cannot develop any culture as long as he remains in this paradise. For Freud, culture is conditioned by the partial non-satisfaction of instinctual desires, which leads in turn to sublimation or reaction formation. Man, then, is confronted with an alternative: total instinctual satisfaction—and barbarism—or partial instinctual frustration, along with cultural and mental development of man. Frequently, however, the process of sublimation fails, and man has to pay the price of neurosis for his cultural development. It must be emphasized that for Freud the conflict that exists between drives and civilization and culture of whatever kind is in no way identical with the conflict between drives and capitalistic or any other form of "repressive" social structure.[14]

Freud's sympathies are on the side of culture, not the paradise of primitivity. Nevertheless, his concept of history has a tragic element. Human progress necessarily leads to repression and neurosis. Man cannot have both happiness and progress. In spite of this tragic element, however, Freud remains an enlightenment thinker, though a skeptical one, for whom progress is no longer an unmixed blessing. In the second phase of his work, after the first World War, Freud's picture of history became truly tragic. Progress, beyond a certain point, is no longer simply bought at great expense, but is in principle impossible. Man is only a battlefield on which the life and death instincts fight against each other. He can never liberate

[14]Herbert Marcuse, who represents Freud as a revolutionary thinker and not as a liberal reformer, has tried to give a picture of a state of complete drive satisfaction in a free, in contrast to a repressive, society. Regardless of the validity of his construction, he has failed to state that in this point he negates the essential part of the Freudian system.

himself decisively from the tragic alternative of destroying others or himself.

Freud tried to mitigate the harshness of this thesis in an interesting letter to Einstein, "Why War?" But in his essential position, Freud, who called himself a pacifist at that time, did not allow himself to be seduced either by his own wishes, or by the embarrassment of expressing deep pessimism in the decade of new hope (1920–1930); he did not change or prettify the harshness of what he believed to be the truth. The skeptical enlightenment philosopher, overwhelmed by the collapse of his world, became the total skeptic who looked at the fate of man in history as unmitigated tragedy. Freud could hardly have reacted differently, since his society appeared to him as the best possible one, and not capable of improvement in any decisive way.

In concluding this sketch of Freud's anthropology I should stress that one can best understand the greatness of Freud, that of the man and that of his work, only if one sees him in his fundamental contradictions, and as bound— or chained—to his social situation. To say that all his teachings, over a period of almost fifty years, are in no need of any fundamental revision, or to call him a revolutionary thinker rather then a tragic reformer, will be appealing to many people, for many different reasons. What is required, however, is to contribute to the *understanding* of Freud.

3

MARX'S CONTRIBUTION
TO THE KNOWLEDGE OF MAN

SOME PRELIMINARY REMARKS seem to be in order. Marx's contribution to the knowledge of man or, in a narrower sense, to psychology, is a topic which has found relatively little attention. Quite unlike Aristotle or Spinoza, whose works on ethics are treatises on psychology, Marx is supposed not to have been much concerned with the individual man, his drives, and his character, but only with the laws of society and its evolution.

This disregard of Marx's contribution to psychology is caused by a number of factors. One, that Marx never put his psychological views in any systematic form, but that they are distributed all over his work and have to be pulled together to display their systematic nature. Second, the vulgar misinterpretation of Marx as having been concerned only with economic phenomena, or the misinterpreted concept of historical materialism, according to which Marx assumed that man is by nature driven primarily by the wish for economic gain, obscured Marx's real picture of man and his contribution to psychology. Third, Marx's dynamic psychology came too early to find sufficient attention. It was not until Freud that a systematic depth psychology was developed, and Freud's psychoanalysis became the most important dynamic psychological system. Its popularity, to some extent due to its mechanistic materialism, obscured recognition of the core of the

["Marx's Contribution to the Knowledge of Man" was given as a paper at a Symposium on the influence of Karl Marx on contemporary scientific thought, Paris, May 8–10, 1968, organized under the auspices of UNESCO by the International Social Science Council and the International Council for Philosophy and Humanistic Studies, and is being reprinted from *Social Science Information*, VII, 3, pp. 7–17.]

relative drive. This distinction is closely related to the distinction between human nature in general and its specific manifestations. At this point I only want to say briefly how extraordinarily fruitful this division between fixed and relative drives is, and that this concept alone constitutes a most important contribution to the present-day discussion of drives and instincts. Marx clarifies the distinction still further by saying that "relative appetites" (another word for drives) "are not an integral part of human nature" but "owe their origin to certain social structures and certain conditions of production and communication." Here Marx already linked the relative appetites with social structure and conditions of production, and communication, and thus laid the foundation for a dynamic psychology which understands most human appetites—and that means a large part of human motivation—as being determined by the process of production. The concept of "social character," in the dynamic sense in which I have formulated it, is based on this notion of Marx.

Not less important than Marx's distinction between constant and relative drives is his discussion of the animal versus the human quality of constant drives. And it is precisely at this point that we find the decisive difference between Marx's dynamic psychology and that of Freud. Considering those drives which are "constant" and assumed, by psychoanalysts as well as by academic psychologists, to be of the same quality in man and animals, Marx states that "eating, drinking, and procreating are, of course, also genuine human functions. But abstractly considered, apart from the environment of other human activities, and turned into final and sole ends, they are animal functions." For Freudian psychoanalysis, based on the model of the isolated *homme machine*, whose drives are fed by inner chemical processes, and whose goal is the reduction of tension to an optimal threshold, the satisfactions of hunger, thirst, and sexual desire are, indeed, ends in themselves.

We are now prepared for one of Marx's most fundamental statements concerning the nature of drives: "Passion is man's faculties striving to attain their objects." In this statement passion is considered as a concept of relation, or relatedness. It is not, as in Freud's concept of instinct or drive, an inner, chemically produced striving, which needs an object as a means for its satisfaction, but man's faculties themselves, his *Wesenskraft*, are endowed with the dynamic quality of having to strive for an object they can relate to and unite themselves with. *The dynamism of human nature is primarily rooted in this need of man to express his faculties toward the world, rather than in his need to use the world as a means for the satisfaction of his physiological necessities.* What Marx is saying is that because I have eyes I have the need to see; because I have ears I have the need to hear; because I have a brain I have the need to think; and because I have a heart I have the need to feel. In short, because I am man, I am in need of man and of the world. In passing it might be useful to note, considering the present-day popularity of the so-called psychoanalytic ego psychology, that when Marx speaks here of faculties and their expression, he is precisely not speaking of the ego, but of passion, of "natural powers and faculties which exist in man as tendencies and abilities, as drives"; of the energy invested in the need of each faculty to be expressed.

There are numerous statements by Marx that are variations of the theme of passion as a category of relatedness of man to himself, to others, and to nature and of the realization of his essential powers. Space permits me to quote only a few. Marx makes very clear what he means by "human faculties" which relate to the world in a passionate way: "his *human* relations to the world— seeing, hearing, smelling, tasting, touching, thinking, observing, feeling, desiring, acting, loving—in short, all the organs of his individuality are the ... active expression (*Betätigung*) of human reality." Precisely because the object is an expression of human reality, it, itself, becomes human, or as Marx put it, "in practice I can only relate myself in a human way to a thing when the thing is related in a human way to man." (In passing I should like to call attention to the basic similarity of this concept of Marx with concepts to be found in Goethe, Zen Buddhism, and Christian mysticism.)

Man's "drives," then, are an expression of a fundamental and specifically human need, the need to be related to man and nature, and of confirming himself in this relatedness. The aim is to "accomplish the union of man with nature, the realized naturalism of man and the realized humanism of nature." The need for self-realization in man is the root of the specifically human dynamism. The wealthy man is at the same time one who needs "a complex of human manifestations of life, and whose own self-realization exists as an inner necessity, a need."

Marx also saw clearly the connection between man's relatedness to himself and his relatedness to others. His position in this respect is essentially the same as that of Goethe, who said: "Man knows himself only as much as he knows the world. He knows the world only within himself, and he is aware of himself within the world. Each new object truly recognized opens up a new organ within ourselves." From this concept of dynamic relatedness it follows that for Marx "the wealthy man is at the same time one who *needs* a complex of human manifestations of life, and whose own self-realization exists as an inner necessity, a *need*." Hence "poverty is a passive bond which leads man to experience a need for the greatest wealth, the *other* person."

Is this related man who energetically strives for expression of his faculties, the worker, or the bourgeois of the nineteenth century? If the answer is no—and it *is* "no"— what relevance has Marx's model of human nature for the understanding of man? Is it a man of the golden age of the past, or is it the man of the Messianic vision for the future? The answer is complicated, and leads us directly into one of the most profound and most advanced aspects of Marx's psychological system. In contrast to the concept of mental illness, which can be defined in relative terms as an illness different and graver than the illness of the average man or, from a different standpoint, as an illness which does not prevent man from producing and procreating, Marx visualized the *pathology of normalcy*, the crippledness of the—statistically—normal man, the loss of himself, the loss of his human substance. Thus Marx speaks of the possibility that man may "become lost" in the object if the object has not become a human object— that is to say, that his relationship to the object is not that of active relatedness, often called by him "appropriation." He speaks of man's becoming "mentally and physically dehumanized," or of the "crippled" worker, the "mere fragment of a man" versus the "fully developed individu-

al." If man, Marx reasons, does not relate himself *actively*
to others and to nature, then he loses himself, his drives
lose their human qualities and assume animal qualities,
and we might continue, since he is no animal, he is a sick,
fragmented, crippled human being. This is precisely the
revolutionary and the therapeutic element in Marx's dynamic psychology. Man is potentially not only capable, but
in need, of relating himself to the world, and in order to
be human and to be cured, he needs to restore this
potential of a healthy, and not a pathological form of
human functioning.

Marx's concept of the crippled versus the fully developed man forms the basis for a new and original
concept of neurosis. In an important statement in the
German Ideology he says:

> It is nonsense to believe . . . one could satisfy one passion
> separated from all others without satisfying *oneself*, the
> whole living individual. If this passion assumes an abstract,
> separate character, if it confronts him as an alien power,
> that is . . . as the one-sided satisfaction of a single passion—
> this by no means pertains to consciousness or good will . . .
> but to *being;* not to thought, but to life. It is caused by the
> empirical development and manifestation of life of the in-
> dividual . . . if the circumstances under which this individual
> lives permit him only the one-sided development of one
> quality at the expense of all others . . . the result is that this
> individual achieves only a one-sided, crippled development.

Marx speaks here of alienated passions, of passions which
are satisfied as ends in themselves, without satisfying the
whole human being—that is, which are separated from all
other passions and hence oppose the individual as an alien
power. In an instinctivistic psychology like Freud's, where
normalcy and health are the result of the satisfaction,
precisely, of one instinct, the sexual, such a consideration
would have no place. In a humanistic concept of passions,
in which the energy is generated by the active striving of
all faculties to attain their objects, Marx's statement points
to the nature of neurosis or mental illness. It can be
defined as dominance, and hence alienation of one passion.

The key concept for the understanding of the non-alienated drive is *activity*, or, as Marx originally said, "self-activity." Obviously he does not have in mind "activity" as it is used in contemporary language, as doing something, being busy, etc. It is also different from the activity of animals who construct "only in accordance with the standards and needs of the species to which they belong, while man knows how to produce in accordance with the appropriate standard to the object. Thus man constructs also in accordance with the laws of beauty." Marx's concept of activity is close to that of Spinoza, a creative and spontaneous act, possible only under the condition of freedom. He speaks, for instance, of the "spontaneous activity of human fantasy, of the human brain and heart." This concept of activity becomes particularly clear when Marx speaks in very concrete terms of human passions, particularly that of love. "Let us assume," he writes,

> man to be *man*, and his relation to the world to be a human one. Then love can only be exchanged for love, trust for trust, etc. If you wish to enjoy art you must be an artistically cultivated person; if you wish to influence other people you must be a person who really has a stimulating and encouraging effect upon others. Every one of your relations to man and to nature must be a *specific expression*, corresponding to the object of your will, of your *real individual life*. If you love without evoking love in return, *i.e.*, if you are not able, by the *manifestation* of yourself as a loving person, to make yourself a *beloved person*, then your love is impotent and a misfortune.

Marx expresses this active quality of love most clearly in what he writes in *Die Heilige Familie*: "Mr. Edgar transforms love into a goddess and into a cruel goddess by transforming the loving man or the love of man into the man of love, thus making 'love' a being separated from man. By this simple process, the transformation of predicate into subject" man is transformed into no-man. Indeed, love is a human activity, not passivity (*to be* in love, rather than *to fall* in love) and, Marx says, "it is love which teaches man to truly believe in the world of objects outside of him."

Marx's concept of truly human needs—the need of the other, the need to express and to pour one's faculties into their adequate objects, can be understood fully if one pays attention to Marx's concepts of synthetic, inhuman, and enslaving needs. Modern psychology is little concerned with the critical analysis of needs; it accepts the laws of industrial production (maximal production, maximal consumption, and minimal human friction) by assuming that the very fact a person desires something is proof that he has a legitimate need for the desired thing. Orthodox psychoanalysis, focusing mainly on sexual needs, or, later, on destructive needs, in addition to the needs for survival, had no reason to concern itself with the wider range of needs. Marx, on the other hand, because of the dialectic nature of his psychology, showed the ambiguous character of needs very clearly and, in fact, used this point as his most severe attack against the science of psychology. "What is to be thought of a science," so he says in the *Economic and Philosophical Manuscripts*, "which ... does not feel its own inadequacy, even though this great wealth of human activity means nothing to it except, perhaps, what can be expressed in the single phrase—'need,' 'common need'?" Those "needs" which are not *human* are characterized by Marx very succinctly:

> Every man speculates upon creating a *new* need in another, in order to force him to new sacrifice, to place him in a new dependence, and to entice him to a new kind of pleasure ... Everyone tries to establish over others an *alien* power in order to find there the satisfaction of his own egoistic need. With the mass of objects, therefore, there also increases the realm of alien entities to which man is subjected. Every new product is a new potentiality of mutual deceit and robbery. Man becomes increasingly 'poor' as man ... This shows subjectively, partly in the fact that the expansion of production and of needs becomes an *inegnious* and always calculating subservience to inhuman, depraved, unnatural and *imaginary* appetites.
>
> As a result, ... the production of too many useful things results in too many *useless* people. Both sides forget that prodigality and thrift, luxury and abstinence, wealth and poverty, are equivalent.

With this distinction between genuine and imaginary human needs, Marx's psychology touches upon one of the most important distinctions to be made in the theory of needs and drives. The question how to distinguish between human and inhuman, real and imaginary, helpful and poisonous, needs is, indeed, a fundamental psychological problem that neither psychology nor Freudian psychoanalysis could even begin to investigate, because they made no such distinctions. And how could they make such distinctions when their model is the alienated man, when the fact that modern industry creates and satisfies more and more needs is taken as a sign of progress, and when the contemporary concept of freedom, to a large extent, reflects the freedom of the customer to choose between various and virtually identical brands of the same commodity within the reach of his pocketbook—a freedom of the consumer quite different from the freedom of the entrepreneur in the nineteenth century? Only a dialectical and revolutionary psychology, which sees man and his potentiality beyond the appearance of a crippled man, can arrive at this important distinction between two kinds of needs, the study of which may be initiated by those psychologists who do not mistake the appearance for the essence. It should be noted in passing that Marx, once he had made this distinction, was forced to conclude that poverty and wealth, abstinence and luxury, are not contradictions but equivalents, resting on the frustration of *human* needs.

So far we have dealt with Marx's concepts of drives and needs in a general way. It there anything more specific concerning drives to be found in his psychology? Indeed there is, even though by no means anything as systematic or as complete as we would expect in a work that deals primarily with psychology.

It has already been mentioned that for Marx the concept of love is crucial in describing man's relationship to the outside world. It is crucial also for the process of thinking; one of the main criticisms against "Herr Edgar" in *Die Heilige Familie* is precisely that he tries to get rid of the passion of love in order to find total peace of knowing. In this context Marx equates love with all "that is life, all that is immediate, all sensuous experience, all real experience, of which one never knows beforehand whence and whither." As far as human relations are concerned, Marx believes that "the immediate, natural and necessary relation of human being to human being is the *relation of man to woman* ... The relation of man to woman is the *most natural* relation of human being to human being."

It is very interesting to compare this concept of Marx with the concept of sexuality in Freud. For Freud, sexuality (and in his later work, destructiveness) is a central passion of man. As I have indicated before, this passion is conceived of as the use of woman by man in order to satisfy his chemically produced sexual hunger. Had Marx known Freud's theory he would have criticized it as a typical bourgeois theory of use and exploitation. In the center of Marx's concept of human relations we find not sexuality, but Eros, of which sexuality can be one expression. By Eros is meant here the specifically male-female attraction which is a fundamental attraction in all living substance.

Another basic category in Marx's psychology is that of life as against death, not in a biological-physiological sense, but in a psychological one. (In many ways this concept touches upon Freud's life and death instinct, but without its alleged biological substratum; more directly, it approaches what I have called biophilia and necrophilia—love of life and love of death.) Perhaps the most decisive question in Marx's psychology is whether a man, class, or society is motivated by the affinity to life or to death. His enmity against capitalism, as his love for socialism, as far as their emotional background is concerned, are rooted in this dichotomy. Among the various places where Marx mentioned this distinction, I quote here only the one best known, that in the *Communist Manifesto*: "In bourgeois society living labor is but a means to increase accumulated labor. In Communist society, accumulated labor is but a means to widen, to enrich, to promote the existence of the laborer. In bourgeois society, therefore, the past dominates the present; in Communist society, the present dominates the past." Or, as he put it elsewhere, the rule of capital is "the domination of living men by dead matter." Eros and love of life are the two central strivings of the unalienated man. They are given in human nature, and manifest themselves under social circumstances that give man the possibility to be what he could be. Among the passions that are produced in, and govern man in capitalist society, Marx includes any kind of greed that is a substitute for the lack of love and aliveness, and more specifically acquisitiveness, avarice, and self-indulgence. His analysis of the ascetic, hoarding character of the bourgeois of the ninetenth century and of the self-indulgent character of those who could afford the luxurious life is a milestone in the development of a dynamic characterology applied to various classes. Since Marx's whole psychological thinking is dynamic, and not behavioristic-descriptive, those character traits and character concepts have to be understood in the dynamic sense. They are relatively constant passions and appetites determined by certain economic and social conditions. Marx is related here to the great social-psychological work of Balzac, who considered the study of character to be the study of those "forces by which man is motivated." The work of Balzac is in many ways the elaboration of Marx's psychological principles. It must be added in passing, that if one reads Marx's letters to Engels, especially in their unabridged German original, one finds a depth-psychological view of individuals which, while not having the artistic qualities of Balzac's descriptions, belong among the best psychoanalytic sketches of character in terms of a dialectic humanist psychoanalysis.

This brief resume of Marx's psychology of drives can conclude with his reference to rage; what is especially interesting is his idea that rage can be turned against oneself, an idea that later on played an important part in Freud's psychoanalysis. Marx wrote, "Shame is a kind of rage which is turned against oneself, and if a whole nation were really ashamed, it would be as were it the lion which crouches before it leaps."

Marx's contribution to humanistic depth psychology could not be fully understood without knowing his attitude toward consciousness and his concept of the function of becoming aware. Its classic expression is in the *German Ideology*: "It is not consciousness that determines life, but life that determines consciousness." Later, in the Preface to the *Contribution to the Critique on Political Economy*, he writes, "It is not the consciousness of men that determines their existence, but, on the contrary, it is their social existence that determines consciousness." What he calls in the first statement "life" he calls in the second statement "social existence." Continuing the tradition of which Spinoza was one of the early outstanding exponents, and which found its culmination in Freud over fifty years later, Marx attacks the prevalent opinion that consciousness is the ultimate datum and the quality of all psychic life. Marx saw, and in this respect more deeply than Freud, that consciousness is the product of the particular practice of life which characterizes a given society or class. It is "from the very beginning a social product"; like language, it arises "from the need, the necessity for intercourse with other men. While man thinks he is determined and motivated by his own ideas, he is in reality motivated by forces behind his back and of which he is not aware." While Marx already used the term *repression* (*Verdrängung*) in relation to the repression of "ordinary natural desires," in the *German Ideology*, Rosa Luxemburg quite explicitly, and following Marx's thought, spoke of the dichotomy between the "conscious" and the "unconscious." In an interpretative version of Marx's statement about consciousness being determined by social existence, she writes: "The unconscious comes before the conscious. The logic of the historic process comes before the subjective logic of the human beings who participate in the historic process." In a class society man's consciousness is necessarily false consciousness, ideology, which gives the appearance of the rationality of his actions when due to the contradictions of any class society the true motivations are not rational.

Marx's concept of consciousness and ideology led to one of the most essential parts of his theory of revolution. In a letter of September, 1843, he speaks of consciousness as "a thing which the world must appropriate, although it does not want to do so ... our motto must be then: reform of consciousness not by dogmas but by the analysis of the mythical consciousness unclear to itself, be it religious or political." The destruction of illusions and the analysis of consciousness—that is to say, awareness of the reality of which man is not conscious, are the conditions for social change. Marx has expressed this in many splendid formulations: one must force "the frozen circumstances to dance by singing to them their own melody";

or, "The demand to give up illusions about one's condition is the demand to give up conditions which need illusions." Man should become "a disappointed man who has come to his senses in order that he may move around himself and thus around his real sun." Awareness of reality as a key to change is for Marx one of the conditions of social progress and revolution, as it is for Freud the condition for the therapy for mental illness. Marx, not being interested in problems of individual therapy, did not speak about awareness as a condition for individual change, but considering his whole psychological system, as I have tried to outline it here, it is by no means a tour de force to make this connection.[1]

I believe that when Marx's central concern—with man— has been fully recognized, his contribution to psychology will find the recognition which so far has been denied it.

---

[1] Cf. my detailed presentation of Marx's psychological concepts in *Marx's Concept of Man* (New York, tr. Ungar Publ. Co., 1961) and in *Beyond the Chains of Illusion*, Credo Perspectives, ed. Ruth Nanda Anshen (New York, Simon and Schuster, 1962).

4

HUMANISTIC PLANNING

IN INVESTIGATING AREAS of convergence between business planning and government planning, one quickly realizes that the subject also implies convergence between psychology and social philosophy, on the one hand, and management and planning, on the other. The latter field of convergence includes two important areas; one, rather obvious, is the work of industrial psychologists. Perhaps the most important step, from which all later work followed, was taken by Elton Mayo in his famous experiment in the Hawthorne Plant of General Electric, where he studied the effect on productivity of various devices for manipulating or using the human material involved in labor. Mayo took unskilled women workers, introduced pauses, and other inducements, and the productivity rose. Then he omitted all such inducements, and productivity still rose. Finally he had the idea—which was the insight of a great scientist—that it was not the pause and the other inducements which had not only increased productivity but also decreased absenteeism and induced friendlier human relationship among these workers, but an entirely different factor—the *emergence of interest in what the workers were doing*. They were participating actively and with interest in what they were doing simply because they had been told about the experiment of which they were part, and its meaning, and thus, for the first time, the

["Humanistic Planning" was given as a talk at the TIMS meeting, Los Angeles, California, 1968. Acknowledgment is given to The Institute of Management Sciences for permission to publish it.]

purely mechanical, repetitive, and boring work situation had been transformed into one that interested them. This indeed was the factor that brought about the increase in productivity. With Mayo's experiment the principle was experimentally confirmed that interest in work is a powerful incentive, aside from that of the monetary incentive.

The industrial psychologists who followed Mayo—Likert, McGregor, White, and others—have added new material to Mayo's findings. Perhaps McGregor has drawn the most radical consequences, emphasizing that not only satisfactions of the ego—that is, pride and self-esteem—but also possibly what is so often, since Kent Goldstein, called in modern psychology "self-actualization," or "self-realization," contribute to an increase in the productivity of work.

However, there is one point we must not forget, and that is that all these studies were prompted by the question, "How can one motivate men in order to get better production?" Or, "How should one use the means—human material—in order to enhance the end—a more efficient use of machines?" Or, to put it differently, Professor Mayo entitled his book *The Human Problem of Industry*. He could have given it the title *The Industrial Problem of Man*, but he did not. But the crucial question is: "Who or what is the end and what-or-who is the means?" In the field of industrial psychology it seems that the end is the productivity of labor and that man's development, or what is good for man, is a means to achieve this end. Indeed, many industrial psychologists seem to assume the existence of a kind of preestablished harmony between human and industrial interests, a harmony which assumes that what is best for man is best for industry. I believe that this is true to some extent, but we should ask ourselves, "What if this is not so?" What is our attitude to that challenging sentence in the Bible, "For what is man profited if he shall gain the whole world and lose his soul?" And the text continues, "And what shall man give in exchange for his soul?" The answer, of course, is "The soul has no exchange value."

Despite all the valuable work that industrial psychology has done, I believe that it confuses the issue in this one respect. By assuming this preestablished harmony between the interests of production and the best interests of man, it camouflages the fundamental question, "What are we really concerned with?" Are we primarily concerned with the growth of man, or are we concerned with production, or machines, or the organization?

We are forced to look squarely at an embarrassing contradiction. Our culture is based on the Judaeo-Christian tradition, and we are brought up *believing* in the Ten Commandments and the Golden Rule; nevertheless, we have a *practice* in which almost anybody who operated on the bases of the Ten Commandments and the Golden Rule would be a failure. With some exceptions of course, and especially in certain fields, it is difficult to combine maximal success with obedience to our traditional moral codes. We believe in one set of values, while we act in an opposite direction. I am not a preacher, but it is easy to see for the psychologist that this split within ourselves has rather damaging consequences. A man who lives on this "split level," with one set of values which he respects, and another set of contrary values according to which he acts, suffers from a good deal of guilt feeling that saps his energy, makes him defensive, very often makes him project his own feeling of guilt on others, etc.; it is crucial, therefore, that we acknowledge the conflict we are living. Do we follow the words of Matthew, or the principle that the end of all our efforts is the growth and efficiency of our economic machine?

There is another cautionary note to be made in regard to the work done in industrial psychology. Like most academic psychology, industrial psychology is behavioristically oriented, in contrast to the dynamically oriented depth psychology that is the frame of reference of my own work. Later I will try to explain why this difference is extremely important in regard to the application of psychological methods to management and planning.

The second and more fundamental point of convergence between psychology and management science, however, is between analytic social psychology and the ideas that have been expressed in the philosophy of management, particularly in the work of Ozbekhan and Churchman. They have raised the questions very explicitly: "What are we planning for? What are the values of our planning?" They are reminding us that we must be aware of the norms and values underlying all our planning before we can speak of strategic or even tactical planning.

Closely related to these questions is another, even more fundamental: What do we mean by planning? Do we mean executing a predetermined plan in an ordered fashion, or do we mean the "willing of the future," as Ozbekhan has expressed it? Let us take, as an example, the recent use made of computers in matching presumably compatible marriage partners. Should a prospective bride, who has been matched in this way, say, "We *plan* to marry next month," or "We *are planned* to marry next month"? Indeed, I think this question is relevant not only for that fortunate, or unfortunate, couple, but also to the whole concept of planning in our society. Are *we* really planning, or are we *planned to plan* according to certain principles which we do not question and for which we have no responsibility?

What are these principles that plan our planning? It would seem that the one norm for planning that our technological society had developed is: *one ought to do whatever it is technically possible to do.*[1]

This technological value principle means that if we have the ability to travel to the moon, then we ought to go there, without further ado. Similarly, if we have learned how to construct still more devastating weapons, then we ought to go ahead and construct them. In such a perspective technical feasibility becomes a source of all value formation. If, indeed, the norm becomes simply that which it is technically possible to do, then religious and ethical norms have been abdicated. Our traditional spiritual norms were all based on the idea that one ought to do what is good for man, what is true, what is beautiful, what is conducive to his growth and to his aliveness. If we accept the system of norms that says we ought to do anything that we can technically accomplish, then indeed, while we may still pay lip service to our traditional value system, we have in fact abandoned it. Of course, this technological assumption that "one ought to do what one can do" is not an explicit norm of which we are conscious as a value principle. Nevertheless, it determines our ac-

---

[1] Lewis Mumford had formulated earlier this concept to which Ozbekhan and I had arrived separately.

tion, while in our consciousness we still hold on to the norms of the Judaeo-Christian tradition.

Are we then confronted with an unavoidable collision of the norms of humanism and the commands of technical progress? Fortunately, there is a third possibility for a system of values, not one based on revelation but on our knowledge of man's nature. The basis for this value system lies in the idea that it is possible to determine what is good and what is bad for man if we can come to understand his nature. "Good" and "bad" do not mean here what he desires or does not desire, nor simply what is good or bad for his material well-being; it means what is conducive to the full growth of the total man, of all his capacities and potentialities, what is good for the attainment of his optimal human maturity. Objectively valid norms can be established in this way, without recourse to revelation, and these norms are essentially identical with those common to all the great humanistic religions, like Taoism, Buddhism, Judaism, Christianity, and Islam.[2] Although I cannot demonstrate the feasibility of such norms in this chapter, there is some purpose in adding some explanatory observations that may serve to form a link between the concepts used in systems analysis and those used in psychoanalysis.

Man is a system—like an ecological or political system, the system of the body or of the cell, or a system of society or an organization. In analyzing the system "man," we understand that we are dealing with a system of forces, and not with a mechanical structure of behavior particles. Like any system, the system "man" has great coherence within itself and shows great resistance to change; furthermore, the change of one item that is allegedly "the cause" of another undesirable item will not produce any change in the system as a whole.

The difficulty in understanding the system "man" lies in two directions. First, it meets with the same difficulties which the concept of system finds in common-sensical thought. It requires thinking in terms of processes, and giving up the antiquated cause-effect model of thinking. The other difficulty lies in the fact that for most people it is difficult to acept the idea of forces behind overt

[2] I have tried to outline such a system of humanistic ethics in *Man for Himself*, New York, Holt, Rinehart and Winston, 1947.

behavior. Let me give a very simple example. If you see a man with a red face shouting, and you say, "He is angry," you will be making a true statement. But if you probe into his system more deeply, you might say, "This man is frightened," and if you probe still more deeply, you might decide, "This man feels helpless." Now, all three statements are correct. However, we have a varying degree of relevance, because only the statement "This man feels powerless" comes close to the basic fact with which I am dealing; as long as I see him as an angry man, I see only a surface phenomenon.

The motivating forces are often unconscious. For example, you see a man behind the post office window. It is just six o'clock; there are still three people waiting and he shuts his window. If you are a good observer, you will see just a little flicker of satisfaction on his face over the fact that these three people will have to leave and won't get their stamps. He is not aware of it, but the incident might give you just the hint that, in an entirely different situation—for example, in a regime of terror, this man might be a sadistic torturer. The sadistic trend may show overtly under circumstances that permit him to express it quite openly and perhaps even intensely. Here again we can come to recognize that a certain force, like sadistic desire, may hardly be visible in action or in consciousness, but under certain circumstances it might become a strong force in the system of a particular person.

A further element in this analysis of the system "man" is that it is relatively predictable. It would perhaps be better to say "character" rather than "system man," because we are all familiar with what we mean by "character." Even people who are not professional psychologists have been taught by experience not to assume that the character of a person is identical with the behavior he shows, much less with what he thinks about himself. If we really judge men, we do not judge from what they do at the moment, but we judge certain forces we intuit and which we believe might come to the fore at a later point under certain circumstances. Of course, even with the greatest knowledge one might have, it is not possible to predict the future behavior of a person with certainty, only with probability. But we can predict future mass behavior with a greater degree of certainty if we know the character structure common to a whole group of people.

As a footnote it is worth recalling that in 1932 we were very much interested in how the workers and employees would react to Hitler if and when he came to power. As far as their opinions were known, they were almost one hundred percent against Nazism, but we were convinced that it depended on the relative strength of authoritarian versus anti-authoritarian forces in their character structure, whether they would fight against Hitler, become Nazis themselves once Hitler won, or try to survive, neither as ardent fighters against nor ardent admirers of Hitler. We were able to predict roughly the percentage of individuals who would choose each of these three responses by analyzing the character structure of this group, a prediction later on roughly confirmed by the facts.

My main thesis is simply that the analysis of the system "man" must become an integral part of the analysis of the system "enterprise" or the system "society." In other words, the science of man must become one of the managerial sciences. Even if we disagree on the possibility of constructing objectively valid values on the basis of the knowledge of man, it still remains a fact that we simply do not know what we are doing in our planning unless we understand the system "man" and integrate it into the social and organizational system. Otherwise, we are dealing with the analysis of a social system without taking into consideration one of its most important subsystems. Besides, once we understand the system "man," the difficult problem of determining universal, objectively valid values may lose somewhat in importance. Even if we cannot agree on the validity of a system of rational ethics, we can work out a common answer to the question, "What does a certain system of management do to man?" Once we are aware of the consequences of our planning for man, we can decide whether in view of these consequences we prefer one goal of planning, or one method of management, to another. These consequences—and this is the important point—can be recognized only by the study of the system "man" within the social system the planning refers to. Without knowledge of man we would be apt to imagine results that justify our favorite method of planning, but which are fictitious. However, it is important not to restrict ourselves to the question, "What are the consequences for human behavior of a certain way of planning or management during the seven or eight hours of work?" but also to ask, "What are its consequences for human behavior *outside* of the work situation?"

Let us think of a specific example, a blue-collar worker with a repetitive job. He is bored, resentful, and angry. Actually, his job gives him no pleasure, but he is compensated for the unpleasure of his job by the consumption he can indulge in during the rest of the day when he is already tired, or on weekends. However, this consumption has its limitations, which are quite irritating. He lives in a world in which much more is advertised than he is able to consume. In spite of his splendid standard of living, as compared with the workers in the rest of the world, subjectively speaking, he is rather restricted in his consumption. We hear him complaining about taxes, or Negroes moving into his neighborhood, or about the fear of losing his job. What effect does his underlying resentment and anger have on his relationship to his wife and his children? What does it do to his function as a citizen? Is he not eventually brought into a situation where he easily falls prey to a demagogue who appeals to his resentment and exploits it for purposes that have nothing to do with the interests of this blue-collar worker? What I am trying to say is simply that if you create certain effects in the system of work you may seem to be managing quite successfully, but you may also be creating defects in the system "man," both individually and socially, which outweigh the advantages for the enterprise and for that the whole society pays, materially and morally. Only a thoughtful and analytical study of the structure of man can show what the *total* effects of a certain kind of planning and management really are.

Eventually, of course, you may arrive at the concept of norms which are objectively valid from the standpoint that is quite familiar to those who deal with systems. If you ask, "What is the optimal functioning of the system 'man'?" you might answer, "It means the optimal development of all his faculties, minimal friction and waste of energy within man, between man and man, and between man and his environment."

One or two examples may indicate more concretely what is meant by this general principle. Man has a need to be close to others. This closeness can assume several forms—for instance, the closeness of a submissive person to the one on whom he is dependent. In this case the price for closeness is a lack of independence, lack of judgment, or rebellious tendencies, although often unconscious ones, against the person on whom he depends. This closeness based on submission stunts the individual's full development and creates deep frictions within him, especially because of the conflict between submission and rebellion.

There is only one form of closeness that does not stunt development and does not cause friction or waste of energy, and that is mature love; by this I refer to the full intimacy between two persons, with each retaining his full independence, and, in a certain sense, his separateness. Love is intrinsically not conflictive and not energy-wasting, because it combines two profound human needs: closeness and independence. Other examples would be the proper balance between intellectual and emotional forces, between the principle of unconditional all-forgiving charity and the principle of responsibility and structure. Many more examples could be given that would confirm the fact that the very nature of the system "man" is such that certain solutions are conducive to optimal functioning and others to wasteful dysfunctioning. The latter situation, of course, is clearly to be seen in the pathology of neuroses and psychoses; one must not forget, however, the "pathology of normalcy," the culturally patterned defects that are manifestations of systemic dysfunctioning but which, being shared by many or most of the members of a society, are not experienced as pathological.

It is perfectly feasible with our present knowledge of the system "man" to design a model of character structure that is conducive to optimal functioning and minimal waste of energy. Such a model would permit the formulation of objectively valid values. In fact, both Aristotle and Spinoza designed such models, although in different terms from the one suggested here. Freud, while not dealing with the problem of values explicitly, implicitly established certain values that would be most conducive to optimal human functioning.

Integrated planning, therefore, requires integration of the system "man" into the system "enterprise-government-society." It is quite possible that one might find that something which is economically efficient may be humanly, and hence socially, detrimental, and we must be prepared to make choices between our real ends—either the maximal unfolding of man or the maximal growth of production and consumption. We can make such choices only if we stop believing that there is a preestablished harmony between the two, or, speaking in traditional religious language, that the interests of God are identical with the interests of Caesar. In fact, there is a good deal of evidence to show that we in the United States and the whole Western industrialized world—which includes, as I believe, the Soviet Union—find ourselves in a severe crisis which is not so much economic, but a human crisis. We see a growth in violence, boredom, anxiety, and isolation, and our increasing consumption does not seem to be sufficient to satisfy man's hunger to be doing more than just reproducing himself and having material satisfaction.

Is there a way out of this human crisis? We might perhaps better ask, do we need to produce defects in the system "man" in order to have an efficient system of management and economic production? Or, do we need to produce sick men in order to have a healthy economy? I have no doubt that it is possible to build an industrial society centered on the full development of man, and not on maximal production and consumption. But this would mean a radical change in our social structure, in our overall goals, in the priorities of production and in our methods of managing. Whether we shall be able to make these changes and thus avoid the danger of disintegration is very uncertain indeed. There are, however, a few factors that furnish some hope. First of all, we have the material means and techniques, as well as the theoretical knowledge and insight, to humanize the technological society. Second, there is an increasing demand for such humanization, not only among so-called hippies and radical students, but among those Americans who have not forgotten the humanist tradition, whose conscience and concern are not dead, and who have become more and more aware that our way of life is conducive to painful boredom. I believe that the increasing awareness of the human consequences of our type of social organization, and our valueless planning, may be, indeed, a critical factor for the survival of our civilization.

5

THE OEDIPUS COMPLEX:
COMMENTS ON THE CASE OF LITTLE HANS

By 1905 FREUD had published his *Three Essays on the Theory of Sexuality*. His data, obtained from the study of the analyses of adults, awoke in him the scientific need of proving the validity of his observations, by reviewing directly the material drawn from a child's life. As a result of this concern, he published, four years later the "Analysis of a Phobia in a Five-Year-Old Boy," a work full of fruitful concepts, which seemed to Freud to prove the pathogenic role of the Oedipus complex.

Freud thought that Hans already "really was a little Oedipus."[1] Little Hans felt great pleasure at being in bed with his mother and going to the bathroom with her. On the other hand he saw in his father a rival. First, in Gmunden, he wanted his father to go away, and later, in Vienna, "the wish had taken the form that the father should be 'dead.'"[2] "The fear which sprang from this death-wish against his father, and which may thus have been said to have had a normal motive, formed the chief obstacle to the analysis until it was removed during the conversation in my consulting-room."[3]

For Freud, Hans's phobias were a consequence of his

[This paper is based on discussions held at the Mexican Institute of Psychoanalysis by a group consisting, aside from the author, of Drs. Fernado Narváez Manzano, Victor F. Saavedra Mancera, Leonardo Santarelli Camelo, Jorge Silva García and Eduardo Zajur Dip.]

[1]Sigmund Freud, "Analysis of a Phobia in a Five-Year-Old Boy" (1909), in *Standard Edition of the Complete Psychological Works of Sigmund Freud*, ed. J. Strachey, London, The Hogarth Press, 1955, X.
[2]*Ibid*, p. 112.
[3]*Ibid*.

libidinal incestuous desire for his mother, exacerbated by his little sister's birth—the event that caused him to be exiled from the parental bedroom and brought about the decrease of maternal attentions. To these must be added his hate for his father as a rival, his fear of the latter's castrating reprisals, and little Hans's longing to continue to be deserving of affection. He desires his father's death and dreads being castrated by him; this dread is symbolically manifested by the fear of being bitten by a horse. Thus, the fright the little boy experiences on seeing a fallen horse is an expression of his death wish against his father. His striving to avoid seeing a horse is a manifestation of the phobia that developed as an escape from both fears.

In spite of the logic and plausibility of Freud's argument, and of his wealth of clinical material, some questions and doubts arise. The first question: Are Hans's parents truly as positive as Freud claims they are in their behavior toward the child?

> His parents were both among my closest adherents, and they had agreed that in bringing up their first child they would use no more coercion than might be absolutely necessary for maintaining good behavious. And, as the child developed into a cheerful, goodnatured and lively little boy, the experiment of letting him grow up and express himself without being intimidated went on satisfactorily.[4]

And Freud adds:

> considering the education given by his parents, which consisted essentially in the omission of "our usual educational sins."[5] Undoubtedly they "were determined from the very beginning, that he was neither to be laughed at nor bullied . . ."[6]

But is it true that little Hans's parents used minimum coercion and that they avoided "our usual educational sins"? Freud, ever the sincere thinker, always offers us undistorted data and gives us sufficient material to demonstrate that his assessment of the parents' attitude is not correct.

[4]*Ibid.*, p. 6.
[5]*Ibid.*, p. 103.
[6]*Ibid.*, p. 117.

1. The educational method of the parents is by no means lacking in threats. The mother menaces him very explicitly with castration. "If you do that [touch his penis with his hand], I shall send for A. to cut off your widdler..."[7] She also threatens to abandon him. Hans: "Mummy's told me she won't come back."[8]

2. Lies also enter into their educational method. We must add that lying to a child is in no way as innocent an act as most parents believe it to be. In the first place, a lie is a subtle form of making fun of the child, especially if he can sense it—though he cannot be sure that the adult's statement is not true. In the second place, lying to a child is another means of using force; the child has no way of knowing what is the truth; he must trust his parents' sincerity, and has no way of defending himself against an untruth. Freud himself has said, "For a small child his parents are at first the only authority and the source of all belief."[9]

In our opinion, Hans is not as naive as his mother believes. Is the child really convinced that the stork brings babies?[10] Freud tells us: "it was parody, it was Hans's revenge upon his father. It was as much as to say: 'If you really expect me to believe that the stork brought Hanna in October, when even in the summer, while we were travelling to Gmunden, I'd noticed how big Mother's stomach was—then I expect you to believe my lies.' "[11]

The same mechanism probably functions in relation to another lie. Hans's mother says that she too has a penis, and his father confirms this. There are reasons to doubt that Hans is quite convinced. We believe that, when he answers that his mother's penis is as large as that of the horse, he is semi-consciously making fun of her.

We shall not continue with examples of the parents' educational method. At this point, we prefer to ask one question: How could Freud have thought that they avoided the usual mistakes when actually they used the same punitive and bullying methods employed by nearly all parents (more mildly and covertly in the middle and upper classes, more harshly and openly in the lower)?

[7]*Ibid.*, p. 7.
[8]*Ibid.*, p. 8.
[9]Sigmund Freud, "Family Romances" (1909), *Collected Papers*, London, The Hogarth Press, 1950, V, p. 74.
[10]Freud, "Analysis of a Phobia in a Five-Year-Old Boy," *op. cit.*, p. 10
[11]*Ibid.*, pp. 70–71.

Truly, the only explanation we can find is that Freud had a "blind spot." His attitude toward bourgeois society was one of liberal, not radical criticism.[12] He wanted to reduce and soften the degree of severity in educational methods, but he did not go so far as to criticize the basis of bourgeois society: the principle of force and threat. The fact that he modified his initial theory about children's traumas is probably to be accounted for by the same attitude. Freud finally arrived at the conclusion that these traumas generally have no basis in fact but are, rather, manifestations of the incestuous and aggressive fantasies of the child. In our opinion, the emphasis given to the incestuous desires of the child is, up to a point, a defense of the parents, who are thus absolved of their incestuous fantasies and the actions that are known to occur. (In Hans's case, as we shall soon see, the mother plays the part of an active seducer.)

Going back now to the clinical material, we are faced with the meaning of little Hans's symptoms. Hans undoubtedly was afraid of castration. But this fear is not based on "very slight allusions," as Freud states. On the contrary, they are clear, strong threats. But where do those threats come from? They are not made by the father but, rather, by the mother. We must consequently deduce that the dread of castration originates with Hans's mother, not with his father. His mother not only terrorizes him with castration, but also tells him (see above) that she will abandon him. His fear of his mother is also manifested by another symptom. "In the big bath I'm afraid of falling in." Father: "But Mummy bathes you in it. Are you afraid of Mummy dropping you in the water?" Hans: "I'm afraid of her letting go and my head going in."[13]

There can be no doubt but that Hans's true apprehensions are caused by the mother, not by the father.

Nor does the little boy's dream about the plumber necessarily suggest that the fear of castration relates to the father, nor even that it expresses fear of castration. It is at least as probable that the dream manifests Hans's desire to

[12]Freud's attitude toward bourgeois society is clearly discernible in his views during World War I. Cf. E. Fromm. *Sigmund Freud's Mission*, World Perspectives, ed. Ruth Nanda Anshen, New York, Harper & Row, 1959.
[13]Freud, "Analysis of a Phobia in a Five-Year-Old Boy," *op. cit.*, p. 67.

have a penis as large as his father's and to be able to exchange his small penis for a larger one. In other words, this fantasy may express his wish to be grown-up rather than the dread of being castrated.

We do not have enough space, within the scope of the present paper, to discuss the fact that Freud's idea—that the child especially fears his father—reflects another of Freud's "blind spots," based on his extreme patriarchal attitude. Freud could not conceive that the woman could be the main cause of fear. But clinical observation amply proves that the most intense and pathogenic fears are indeed related to the mother; by comparison, the dread of the father is relatively insignificant.[14]

Instead of fear of the father, we discover the contrary: It seems that Hans needs his father to protect him from the menacing mother and that the success of the therapy is due not so much to the interpretations as to the protective role of the father and that of the "super-father"—that is, Professor Freud himself.

Classically, the basis of the Oedipus complex is found in the child's incestuous desire for his mother. Freud believed that these desires are "endogenous"—not the result of maternal seduction. We do not doubt that a five- or six-year-old child has sexual interests and desires and that their object is very often the child's mother. Nevertheless, we question whether this sexual desire is as intense and exclusive as Freud considered it to be and, moreover, whether it can be as spontaneous as Freud thought in the absence of active seduction on the mother's part.

The clinical material presented by Freud gives us some important evidence for answering these questions. About the maternal seduction, there can be little doubt but that Hans's mother liked to have him in her bed and to take him with her to the bathroom. But, despite this seductive behavior, the mother is not the exclusive object of sexual attraction for Hans. He wants very much to sleep with Mariedl, and says frankly on one occasion that he prefers her company to his mother's. Hans does feel sexual attraction to her, but not so exclusively and intensely as to give rise to tremendous hate of his father, and consequently to great fear of him.

[14] Cf. J. Silva García, "Man's Fear of Woman," *Revista de Psicoanálisis, Psiquiatría y Psicología*, Fondo de Cultura Económica, I, 2.

This is not to underestimate the importance of the son's fixation upon his mother. On the contrary, we are convinced that this fixation was much deeper than if it had been based mainly or exclusively on sexual desire. The fact is that, usually, sexual interest alone is not the basis for a very constant sexual relationship. He can easily change the objects of his sexual interest, and the same holds true for little boys. Freud suggested that the genital fixation to mother was preceded by pregenital ties.

A child's first erotic object is the mother's breast that nourishes it; love has its origin in attachment to the satisfied need for nourishment . . . This first object is later completed into the person of the child's mother, who not only nourishes it but looks after it and thus arouses in it a number of other physical sensations pleasurable and unpleasurable. By her care of the child's body she becomes its first seducer. *In these two relations* lies the root of a mother's importance, unique, without parallel, established unalterably for a whole lifetime as the first and strongest love-object and as the prototype of all later love-relations—for both sexes.[15]

The emotional bond between the child and the mother, in fact, goes deeper than what is conveyed by the term *pregenital fixation*. It is an affectionate bond of great profundity, a bond in which the mother represents warmth, help, protection; in fact, it stands for life itself, all that is needed to live and to avoid anguish. The mother's love is an unconditional love that generates intense satisfaction, even euphoria.

If Hans's central fear is directed toward his mother rather than his father, how do we explain Hans's phobia? We suggest that the elements that enter into the phobia are as follows: As Hans is already attached to the mother, his terror of her increases with the threats of castration and abandonment. His fear is intensified by his first confrontation with death; before the emergence of his phobia, little Hans witnessed a funeral in Gmunden. Later, he saw a fallen horse and believed it to be dead. The first encounter with death is a very serious event in a child's life, and

[15]Sigmund Freud, "An Outline of Psychoanalysis" (1938), in *Standard Edition*, London, The Hogarth Press, 1964, XXLLL, p. 188.

it can produce additional anguish in an already sensitive child, owing to the fear of castration.

It may therefore be concluded that the fear of the horse has two origins: (1) the fear of the mother, due to her castration threats, and (2) the fear of death. To avoid both fears, Hans develops the phobia, which protects him from seeing horses and from experiencing both types of anxiety.

We are prone to assume on the high probability that his fear of the dray horses hitched to moving vans, and the like, related specifically to the mother, instead of, as in Freud's interpretation, to the father. Is there perhaps an intense but repressed hostile aggression against the mother, due to her threats and her "treason" at giving birth to a daughter—a rival—and also to the little boy's desire to free himself from his fixation on her? This is possible, but there is not enough material to prove it.

There is, however, a fact that supports this hypothesis. Referring to a fantasy of Hans's about a horse he took out of the stable, his father asks him: "You took it out of the stables?" Hans: "I took it out because I wanted to whip it." Father: "Which would you really like to beat? Mummy, Hanna or me?"

Hans: "Mummy."

Father: "Why?"

Hans: "I should just like to beat her."

Father: "When did you ever see anyone beating their Mummy?"

Hans: "I've never seen anyone do it, never in all my life."

Father: "And yet you'd just like to do it?"

Hans: "With a carpet-beater." (His mother often threatened to beat him with the carpet-beater.)[16]

This dialogue suggests the identification of the horse with the mother, and the hostility toward her. Freud considers the possibility of an obscure, sadistic desire for the mother,[17] but he believes that the other element is "a clear impulse for revenge against his father."[18] The latter is the basis for the dominant interpretation in Hans's analysis. But is it a fact that the hostility is directed young through great books that never grow old. These books include Utopia by Thomas More; the complete works of Shakespeare; Benjamin Franklin's Autobiography; Omar Khayyam's Rubaiyat; Walden by Thoreau; and other fresh, spontaneous, even outspoken works that stretch your mind and sweep away the mental cobwebs that hold back most men.

You never have to buy any of these books. (To force you to buy a classic would be barbaric.) As a member, take only those books you really want to own. And, at any time, you may cancel your membership, without penalty or hurt feelings.

(Continued on other side) →

against the father, as Freud concludes? Is that established by any of Hans's affirmations?

In examining the evidence Freud offers in support of this thesis, we must bear in mind that he himself made suggestions to little Hans before having sufficient material to support them: "Finally I [Freud] asked him whether by 'the black round the mouth' he meant a moustache; and then disclosed to him that he was afraid of his father, precisely because he was so fond of his mother."[19] Considering the authority of the professor as "super-father," this suggestion must have had a great deal of influence upon the child. We would ask: To what extent are some of Hans's associations due to this suggestion, and to what extent are they spontaneous?

The feelings of agressivity toward the father are clearly reflected in the following dialogue:

Father: "Then why do you always cry whenever Mummy gives me a kiss? It's because you're jealous." (Note once more the suggestive nature of the interpretation.)

Hans: "Jealous, yes."

Father: "You'd like to be Daddy yourself."

Hans: "Oh yes."

Father: "What would you like to do if you were Daddy?"

Hans: "And you were Hans? I'd like to take you to Linz every Sunday—no, every week-day too. If I were Daddy I'd be ever so nice and good."

Father: "But what would you like to do with Mummy?"

Hans: "Take her to Linz, too."

Father: "And what besides?"

Hans: "Nothing."

Father: "Then why were you jealous?"

Hans: "I don't know."[20]

And later:

Father: "Did you often get into bed with Mummy at Gmunden?"

Hans: "Yes."

Father: "And you used to think to yourself you were Daddy?"

Hans: "Yes."

[19] Ibid., p. 42.
[20] Ibid., p. 89.

Father: "And then you felt afraid of Daddy?"

Hans: "You know everything; I didn't know anything."

Father: "When Fritzl fell down you thought: 'If only Daddy would fall down like that!' And when the lamb butted you, you thought: 'If only it would butt Daddy!' Can you remember the funeral at Gmunden?"

Hans: "Yes. What about it?"

Father: "You thought then that if only Daddy were to die you'd be Daddy."

Hans: "Yes."[21]

Does this conversation attest that Hans feels deep hostility for his father? Of course, if one interprets it with the conviction that it expresses the Oedipus complex, that is the correct interpretation; what Hans says seems to affirm it. But one who studies the material without that conviction arrive at other conclusions: Hans's yearning to take his father's place is not necessarily an expression of hate, or of serious desire for his father's death. We must not forget that one of the most common wishes of children is to be grown-up, not to be subjected any longer to the superior power of adults, not to be an object of fun. That is why little girls want to play with dolls, and little boys imagine they are already adults. Another universal tendency that must also be taken into account is that of experiencing as an active subject what is being experienced as a passive object. In *Beyond the Pleasure Principle*, Freud refers to the general tendency to transform passive into active principles:

> At the outset he was in a passive situation—he was overpowered by the experience; but by repeating it, unpleasurable though it was, as a game, he took on an active part. . . .

> As the child passes over from the passivity of the experience to the activity of the game, he hands on the disagreeable experience to one of his playmates and in this way revenges himself on a substitute.[22]

As Freud has pointed out, clinical experience indicates that the tendency to transform a passive situation into an active one is a powerful force that generates many desires

[21] *Ibid.*, p. 90.

[22] Sigmund Freud, "Beyond the Pleasure Principle" (1920), in *Standard Edition*, London, The Hogarth Press, 1955, XVLLL, pp. 16–17.

in the child as well as in the adult. The wish to be the father, to do actively what is being experienced passively, and moderate jealousy of the father could satisfactorily explain Hans's statements, without supporting the hypothesis of tremendous hostility toward his father as the cause of his anxiety and, indirectly, his phobia.

Another factor should be taken into account. If a five-year-old child says, "Yes, I want my father to die," these words do not necessarily express hate. They may, rather, express a fantasy of something that might seem pleasant at the time, without the intense weight of the realistic idea of death. Hans's analysis tends to indicate that he was neither very afraid of nor hated his father. Had he done so, he would not have spoken so openly to him; nor would he have reacted as positively to the father's questions. If we study the relationship between Hans and his father, without the premise of the Oedipus complex, we can clearly see that it is a relationship based on friendship and confidence.

The question arises: How does one account for the cure of the phobia by means of partially incorrect interpretations? We suggest the following considerations:

1. The erroneous interpretation touches upon *part* of the central conflict, even though only marginally and symbolically.

2. In spite of the fact that the interpretation is not correct, the method of seeking something that exists behind manifest behavior is a help in itself.

3. It is possible that in some cases, as in this one, there is some influence in suggestions: The professor is going to help you clear up your nonsense. Even more so if the professor in question possesses the prestige and authority that Freud had and, what is more, responds with the affection and respect that he showed for Hans throughout the course of the case.

4. Probably the most important factor, if we are correct in assuming that Hans was mainly afraid of his mother, was the interest and support given him by his father and the professor, which encouraged the child, and made him feel stronger and less anxious.

5. Finally, this was a slight phobia, such as occurs in many children, and that it would probably have disap-

peared by itself without any treatment or without the
father's support and interest.

To sum up: it seems that Freud, influenced by his bias
in favor of parental authority and of male superiority,
interpreted the clinical material in a onesided way, and
failed to account for a number of data which contradict
his interpretation.

6

THE SIGNIFICANCE
OF THE THEORY OF MOTHER RIGHT
FOR TODAY

THE FACT THAT Bachofen's theories of Mother Right and the matriarchal societies found relatively little attention in the nineteenth century and the first half of the twentieth is sufficiently explained by the circumstance that up to the end of the first World War the patriarchal system in Europe and America had remained unshaken, so that the very idea of women as the center of a social and religious structure seemed unthinkable and absurd. By the same token, the social and psychological changes that have taken place in the last four decades should provide the reason why the problem of matriarchate should arouse new and intense interest; only now, it seems, are changes occurring which call for a new evaluation of ideas that had remained dormant for over a hundred years. Before writing about these changes, however, let me give the reader not familiar with Bachofen and Morgan a brief introduction to their view of the principles and values of matriarchal society.[1]

According to Bachofen, the matriarchal principle is that of life, unity and peace. The woman, in caring for the infant, extends her love beyond her own self to other

[1] Chapter 7 presents a more detailed discussion of the theory of matriarchy and its psychological significance. Other aspects of the subject are dealt with in E. Fromm, *The Forgotten Language* (New York: Holt, Rinehart and Winston, 1951) in the chapters "The Oedipus Myth and the Oedipus Complex."

human beings, and projects all her gifts and imagination to the aim of preserving and beautifying the existence of another human being. The principle of matriarchy is that of universality, while the patriarchal system is that of restrictions. The idea of the universal brotherhood of man is rooted in the principle of motherhood, but vanishes with the development of patriarchal society. Matriarchate is the basis of the principle of universal freedom and equality, of peace and tender humaneness. It is also the basis for principled concern for material welfare and worldly happiness.[2]

Quite independently, L. H. Morgan came to the conclusion[3] that the kingship system of the American Indians—similar to that found in Asia, Africa, and Australia, was based on the matriarchal principle, and he asserted that the higher forms of civilization "will be a repetition, but on a higher level, of the principles of liberty, equality and fraternity which characterized the ancient *gens.*" Even this brief presentation of these principles of matriarchate should make clear why I attach such importance to the following social-psychological changes:[4]

1. The *failure of the patriarchal-authoritarian system* to fulfill its function; its inability to prevent large and devastating wars and terroristic dictatorships; its incapacity to act in order to prevent future catastrophes, such as nuclear-biological-chemical war, starvation in large parts of the colonial world, and the catastrophic results of increasing poisoning of air, water and soil.

2. The *democratic revolution*, which has defeated the traditional authoritarian structures, and replaced them by democratic structures. The process of democratization has gone together with the emergence of a technological, affluent society that does not mainly require personal obedience but operates, rather, on the basis of teamwork and manipulated consent.

3. The *women's revolution*, which, although not complete, has gone a long way in carrying out the radical

[2] See J. J. Bachofen, *Myth, Religion, and Mother Right*, Princeton, N. J., Princeton University Press, ed. Joseph Campbell, 1968, pp. 69–121.
[3] Tentatively, in his *Systems of Consanguinity and Affinity*, 1871, and more definitely in *Ancient Society*, 1877.
[4] These remarks are merely intended as an introduction to the following chapter, itself a translation of an earlier paper. I am therefore deliberately brief, and shall only mention the changes as such, leaving a more detailed analysis for another occasion.

ideas of the Enlightenment about the equality of men and women. This revolution has dealt a severe blow to patriarchal authority in the capitalist countries as well as in a country as conservative as the Soviet Union.

4. The *children's and adolescents' revolution*: In the past, children were able to rebel only in inadequate ways—refusing to eat, crying, constipation, bed wetting, and general obstinacy, but since the nineteenth century they have found spokesmen (Pestalozzi, Freud, and others) who stressed that children have a will and passions of their own and must be taken seriously. This trend continued with increasing force and insight in the twentieth century, and Dr. Benjamin Spock became its most influential spokesman. As far as adolescents and post-adolescents are concerned, they now speak for themselves—and no longer in a subdued voice. They demand the right to be heard, to be taken seriously, to be active subjects and not passive objects in the arrangements governing their lives. They attack patriarchal authority directly, vigorously—and sometimes viciously.

5. The *vision* of the *consumer's paradise*. Our consumer culture creates a new vision: If we continue on the path of technological progress, we shall eventually arrive at a point where no desire, not even the ever-newly created ones, remains unfulfilled; fulfillment will be instant and without the need to exert any effort. In this vision, technique assumes the characteristics of the Great Mother, a technical instead of a natural one, who nurses her children and pacifies them with a never-ceasing lullaby (in the form of radio and television). In the process, man becomes emotionally an infant, feeling secure in the hope that mother's breasts will always supply abundant milk, and that decisions need no longer be made by the individual. Instead, they are made by the technological apparatus itself, interpreted and executed by the technocrats, the new priests of an emerging matriarchal religion,[5] with Technique as its goddess.

[5] It is important to note that these anti-patriarchal and matriarchal trends occur especially in that sector of the population that is part of the affluent society and working in the cybernated sector. The old lower and middle classes—the peasants, small-town storekeepers, et al., who do not benefit from consumption affluence and feel that their values and identities are threatened, cling fiercely to the old patriarchal and authoritarian order and become violent enemies of the new tendencies, particularly of the groups which express the new values and styles most articulately and radically. (A parallel phenomenon was to be seen in

6. Certain matriarchal tendencies can also be observed in some sectors of the—more or less—radical youth. Not only because they are strictly anti-authoritarian; but also because of their embracing of the above-mentioned values and attitudes of the matriarchal world, as described by Bachofen and Morgan. The idea of group sex (whether in its middle class, suburban forms or in radical communes with shared sex) has a close connection with Bachofen's description of the early matriarchal stage of mankind. The question can also be raised as to whether the tendency to diminish sexual differences in appearance, dress, etc., is not also related to the tendency to abolish the traditional status of the male, and to make the two sexes less polarized, leading to regression (emotionally) to the pregenital stage of the infant.

There are other traits which tend to support the assumption that there is an increasing matriarchal trend among this section of the young generation. The "group" itself seems to assume the function of the mother; the need for immediate satisfaction of desires, the passive-receptive attitude which is most clearly indicated in the drug obsession, the need for huddling together and for touching each other physically—all seem to indicate a regression to the infant's tie to mother. In all these respects the young generation does not seem to be as different from their elders as they think themselves to be, although their consumption patterns have a different content and their despair is expressed overtly and aggressively. The disturbing element in this neo-matriarchialism is that it is a mere negation of patriarchalism and a straight regression to an infantile pattern, rather than a dialectical progression to a higher form of matriarchalism. H. Marcuse's appeal to the young seems to rest largely on the fact that he is the spokesman for infantile regression to matriarchalism and that he makes this principle more attractive by using revolutionary rhetoric.

7. Perhaps not unrelated to these social changes is a development in psychoanalysis that is beginning to correct Freud's older idea about the central role of the *sexual*

---

the same classes in pre-Nazi Germany, and they were the soil from which Nazism grew.)

In Chapter 8, written in German in 1932, I indicated briefly the likelihood of the change from the patriarchal to a matriarchal structure of society.

bond between son and mother, and the resulting hostility toward the father, with the new notion that there is an early "preoedipal" intense bond between the infant and the mother, regardless of the child's sex. In Chapter 1, I indicated how this development began in Freud's later writings, and was taken up by others, although very gingerly. Bachofen's work, if thoroughly studied by psychoanalysts, will prove to be of immense value for the understanding of this nonsexual mother fixation.

I want to conclude these introductory remarks with a theoretical consideration. As the reader will see in the following chapter, the matriarchal principle is that of unconditional love, natural equality, emphasis on the bonds of blood and soil, compassion and mercy; the patriarchal principle is that of conditional love, hierarchical structure, abstract thought, man-made laws and the state.

It seems that in the course of history the two principles have sometimes clashed with each other violently and that sometimes they formed a synthesis (for instance, in the Catholic Church, or in Marx's concept of socialism). If they are opposed to each other, the matriarchal principle manifests itself in motherly overindulgence and infantilization of the child, preventing its full maturity; fatherly authority becomes harsh domination and control, based on the child's fear and feelings of guilt. This is the case in the relationship of the child to father-mother in the family as well as in the spirit of patriarchal and matriarchal societies which determine the family structure. The purely matriarchal society stands in the way of the full development of the individual, thus preventing technical, rational, artistic progress. The purely patriarchal society cares nothing for love and equality; it is only concerned with man-made laws, the state, abstract principles, obedience. It is beautifully described in Sophocles' *Antigone* in the person and system of Creon, the prototype of a fascist leader.[6]

When the patriarchal and matriarchal principles form a synthesis, however, each of the two principles is colored by the other: motherly love by justice and rationality, and fatherly love by mercy and equality.

Today the fight against patriarchal authority seems to be destroying the patriarchal principle, suggesting a return

[6] Cf. the discussion of this point in *The Forgotten Language, op cit.*, "The Oedipus Myth and the Oedipus Complex."

to a matriarchal principle in a regressive and non-dialectic way. A viable and progressive solution lies only in a new synthesis of the opposites, one in which the opposition between mercy and justice is replaced by a union of the two on a higher level.

7

THE THEORY OF MOTHER RIGHT AND ITS RELEVANCE FOR SOCIAL PSYCHOLOGY

BACHOFEN's *Mother Right*, first published in 1861, shared a remarkable destiny with two other scholarly publications that appeared about the same time: Darwin's *Origin of Species* and Marx's *Critique of Political Economy* (both in 1859). All three works dealt with specialized scholarly disciplines, but they brought forth reactions from scholars and laymen far beyond the narrow confines of their own specialty.

As far as Marx and Darwin are concerned, this fact is obvious and calls for no further comment. The case of Bachofen is more complicated, for several reasons. First of all, the problem of matriarchy seems to have far less to do with matters that were vital to the maintenance of bourgeois society. Second, enthusiastic approval of the matriarchy theory came from two camps that were radically opposed to each other both ideologically and politically. Bachofen was first discovered and extolled by the Socialist camp—by Marx, Engels, Bebel, and others. Then, after decades of relative obscurity, he was again discovered and extolled by such anti-Socialist philosophers as Klages and Bäumler.

Over against these two extremes stood the official scholarship of the day, forming practically a solid front of

["The Theory of Mother Right and Its Relevance for Social Psychology" was first published in the *Zeitschrift für Sozialforschung*, Hirschfeld-Leipzig, 1934.]

rejection or outright ignorance—even among such representatives of the Socialist viewpoint as Heinrich Cunow. In recent years, however, the problem of matriarchy has played an ever-increasing role in scholarly discussions. Some agree with the matriarchal view, some reject it; almost all reveal the emotional involvement with the subject.

It is important to understand why the problem of matriarchy arouses such strong emotional reactions and how it is linked up with vital social interests. We also wish to uncover the underlying reasons why the matriarchy theory won sympathy from both the revolutionary and antirevolutionary camps. We can then see the relevance of this problem for the study of present-day social structures and their transformations.

One common element in the opposing attitudes to matriarchy is their common distance from bourgeois-democratic society. Such distance is obviously necessary if one wants to investigate and understand a social structure through the testimony of myths, symbols, legal institutions, etc.—certainly, if this society differs radically from bourgeois society not only in specific aspects but in its basic psycho-social traits. Bachofen himself saw this quite clearly. As he says in the Introduction:

> An understanding of matriarchal phenomena can be achieved only on one condition. The scholar must be able to renounce entirely the ideas of his own time, the beliefs with which these have filled his spirit, and transfer himself to the midpoint of a completely different world of thought. . . . The scholar who takes the attitudes of later generations as his starting point will evidently be turned away from an understanding of the earliest time.[1]

Bachofen's prerequisite was certainly evident in those who rejected their age—whether they looked back to the past as a lost paradise or looked forward hopefully to a better future. But criticism of the present was about the only thing that the two opposing adherents of the matriarchy theory did share. The sharp antagonism between the two groups on every other basic issue suggests that a variety of heterogeneous elements must have been at hand

[1] J. J. Bachofen, op. cit., pp. 81, 82.

in both the matriarchy theory itself and the subject it dealt with. One group could focus on one aspect of the theory as the decisive element, the other group could focus on another aspect; in this way both could find reasons to advocate the theory.

Conservative authors like Bäumler looked backward to the past for their social ideals. What then were the reasons for their particular sympathy for the matriarchy theory?

Engels gives one answer by pointing to—and criticizing—Bachofen's attitude in favor of religion which Bachofen expresses himself clearly:

> There is only one mighty lever of all civilizations, and that is religion. Every rise and every decline of human existence springs from a movement that originates in this supreme sphere.[2]

This attitude is certainly not typical of Bachofen alone. But it is of fundamental importance for his theory, which assumes a close connection between women and religious sentiment:

> If especially matriarchate must bear this hieratic imprint, it is because of the essential feminine nature, that profound sense of the divine presence which, merging with the feeling of love, lends woman, and particularly the mother, a religious devotion that is most active in the most barbarous times.[3]

Bachofen thus sees religious aptitude as the distinctive "disposition" of the female, and religion as a specific trait of matriarchy. Nor does Bachofen regard religion simply as a form of cultic worship and consciousness. One of his most brilliant thoughts is his view that a given structure of the human psyche is related to a specific religion—although he turns the relationship upside down and derives the psychic structure from the religion.

The Romantic aspect of Bachofen's theory shows up even more clearly in his attitude towards the past: he directs his love and attention, in large measure, to the remotest past of mankind, which he idealizes. Even more

[2] *Ibid.*, p. 85.
[3] *Ibid.*

significant, he sees respect for the dead as one of the most basic—and admirable—traits of matriarchal cultures. In his treatment of the Lycian matriarchy, he notes that "the whole life-style of a nation can be seen in its attitude towards the world of the dead. Worship of the dead is inseparable from respect for one's ancestors, and the latter is inseparable from love for tradition and a past-oriented outlook."[4]

Deeply rooted in the maternal-tellurian mystery cults he finds "an emphatic accentuation of the dark, deadly side of nature's life," which is characteristic of the matriarchal outlook. Bäumler clearly points out the difference between the Romantic and the revolutionary outlook in this respect:

> If a person wants to understand myths, he must have a deep feeling for the power of the past. In like manner, if a person wants to understand revolutions and revolutionaries, he must have a profound awareness of the future and its potential.
> To understand the exact nature of this outlook, a person must clearly see that it is not the only possible conception of history. From a deep feeling for the future one may fashion another conception of history—one that involves active, masculine effort, conscious activity, and revolutionary ideals. In the latter framework, man stands free and unshackled in the present and creates the future out of nothing. In the former framework, man is enfolded in the whole "cycle of birth," in the transmission of blood-descent and time-honored customs; he is a member of some "Whole" that loses itself in the unknown recesses of the past . . . The dead will be there, if the living so resolve. They are not dead and gone forever from the earth. All one's ancestors still exist. They continue to advise and act in the community of their descendants.[5]

In Bachofen's conception of the matriarchal psychic structure and the chthonic religion related to it, the decisive feature is the attitude of matriarchal society toward nature, its orientation toward material things as opposed to intellectual and spiritual realities.

[4] *Ibid.*, p. 92.
[5] Cited in J. J. Bachofen, *Der Mythus von Orient und Okzident*, ed. Manfred Schroeder, Munich, 1926, cxii, cxviii.

Matriarchy is bound up with matter and a religious stage of development that acknowledges only corporeal life . . .

The triumph of paternity brings with it the liberation of the spirit from the manifestations of nature, a sublimation of human existence over the laws of material life. While the principle of motherhood is common to all spheres of tellurian life, man, by the preponderant position he accords to the begetting potency, emerges from this relationship and becomes conscious of his higher calling. Spiritual life rises over corporeal existence, and the relationship with the lower spheres of existence is restricted to the physical aspect. Maternity pertains to the physical side of man, the only thing he shares with the animals; the paternal-spiritual principle belongs to him alone. Here he breaks through the bonds of tellurism and lifts his eyes to the higher regions of the cosmos.[6]

Two traits, therefore, characterize the relationship of matriarchal society to nature: passive surrender to nature; and recognition of natural and biological values, as opposed to intellectual ones. Like the mother, nature is the center of matriarchal culture; and mankind ever remains a helpless child in the face of nature.

In the former [i.e., matriarchal culture] we have confinement to matter, in the latter [i.e., patriarchal culture] we have intellectual and spiritual development. In the former we have unconscious lawfulness; in the latter, individualism. In the former we find abandonment to nature; in the latter we find exaltation above nature, a breaking of the old barriers, and the painful strivings of promethean life replacing the constant rest, peaceful pleasure and eternal infantilism in an aging body. The mother's free giving is the exalted hope of the Demeter mystery, which is perceived in the fate of the grain-seed. Hellenic man, on the contrary, wants to win everything, even the most exalted heights, on his own. In struggle he becomes aware of his fatherly nature, and raises himself above maternalism to which he had once completely belonged, and struggles towards his own divinization. No longer does he look for the spring of immortality in the

6 J. J. Bachofen, *Myth, Religion, and Mother Right*, op. cit., pp. 109–110.

child-bearing woman; now he looks for it in the male-creative principle, on which he bestows the divinity that was once accorded only to motherhood.[7]

The value system of matriarchal culture fits in with this passive surrender to mother, nature, and earth and to their central role. Only the natural and biological are worthwhile; the spiritual, cultural, and rational are worthless. Bachofen developed this line of thought most clearly and completely in his concept of justice. In contrast with bourgeois natural law, where "nature" is patriarchal society turned into an absolute, matriarchal natural law is characterized by the dominance of instinctual, natural, blood-based values. In matriarchal law there is no logical, reasonable balancing of guilt and atonement; it is dominated by the "natural" principle of the talion, of returning like for like.

This exclusive respect for the bonds of blood in matriarchal "natural law" is shown most impressively by Bachofen in his interpretation of Aeschylus' *Oresteia*. For the sake of her lover Aegisthus, Clytemnestra slew her husband Agamemnon on his return from the Trojan War. Orestes, the son of Agamemnon and Clytemnestra, avenged this marital murder by slaying his mother. The Erinyes (or Furies), the ancient maternal goddesses who are now overthrown, pursue Orestes for his deed; on the other hand, he is defended by the new divinities of victorious patriarchy, Apollo and Athena, who sprang from the head of Zeus rather than from a mother's womb. What is the essential conflict here? For matriarchal law, there is only one crime: the violation of the blood bond. The Erinyes do not pursue the faithless wife because "she was not related by blood to the man she slew." Infidelity, however foul, does not concern the Erinyes. But when a person violates the ties of blood, no reasoned balancing of justifiable or excusable motivation can spare the doer from the merciless severity of the natural *lex talionis*.

Gynecocracy is "the realm of love and the blood-bond as opposed to the male-apollonian realm of consciously deliberated action."[8] Its categories are "tradition, gener-

---

[7] J. J. Bachofen, *Der Mythos von Orient und Okzident, op. cit.*, p. 49.
[8] Bäumler, as cited in J. J. Bachofen, *Der Mythos von Orient und Okzident, op. cit.*, p. ccxxxiii.

ation, and living interconnectedness through blood and procreation."[9] These categories are used in a concrete sense in Bachofen's work. They are removed from the realm of philosophical speculation and elevated to the realm of scholarly investigation into empirical, ethnological documents, thereby investing the latter with new weight. The vague concepts of nature and the "natural" way of life are replaced by the concrete image of the mother and an empirically demonstrable matricentric legal system.

Bachofen did not simply share the Romanticist's past-oriented and nature-centered outlook. He adopted one of the most fertile ideas of Romanticism as central to his work and developed it far beyond what it had meant in Romantic philosophy. This idea was the distinction between masculine and feminine, which were seen as two qualities that were radically different both in organic nature and in the psychic, spiritual, and intellectual realms. With this conception, the Romantics (and a few representatives of German Idealism) stood in sharp opposition to popular ideas that had been espoused in the seventeenth and eighteenth centuries—especially in France.

The central point of the earlier theories was summed up in the phrase: "Souls have no sex." A whole series of books had examined the man-woman relationship, and the conclusion was always the same. Male and female did not represent qualities that were distinctively imbedded in the intellect and psyche. Whatever psychic differences were to be found between men and women were to be explained simply and solely in terms of their different training and education. It was this factor that made men and women different, even as it made one group different from another in social life.

This earlier notion about the fundamental sameness of the sexes was closely tied up with a political demand, which, made with varying degrees of intensity, played an important role in the era of bourgeois revolution. The demand was the emancipation of woman, her intellectual, social, and political equality. It is easy enough to see how theory and political cause dovetailed in this case. The theory that woman and man were identical formed the basis for demanding her political equality. But whether it was expressed or only implied, woman's equality meant that she, in her very essence, was the same as man in bourgeois society. Emancipation did not mean, therefore, that she was free to develop her specific, as yet unknown, traits and potentialities; on the contrary, she was being emancipated in order to become a bourgeois man. The "human" emancipation of woman really meant her emancipation to become a bourgeois male.

Along with a reactionary political development, there was a change in the theory of the relationship between the sexes and of the "nature" of man and woman. In 1793 women's clubs were shut down in Paris. The theory of basic psychic identity was replaced by the notion that there was a fundamental and unalterable "natural" difference between the sexes.

With the later Romantics, the conception of the fundamental difference between maleness and femaleness was further elaborated by references to historical, sociological, linguistic, mythological, and physiological problems. In contrast to German Idealism and early Romanticism, the meaning of the word "woman" seems to have undergone a change. Whereas formerly "woman" signified her quality as lover, and union with her the experience of authentic "humanness," it came more and more to mean "mother," and the bond with her a return to "nature" and harmonious life in nature's womb.

The Enlightenment had denied sexual differences in the psyche, proclaiming the equality of the sexes, and equating human being with the bourgeois male. This theory was an expression of its efforts to grant social freedom and equality to women. Once bourgeois society had consolidated its gains, and retreated from its progressive political positions, it no longer needed the notion of equality between the sexes. Now it needed a theory propounding the natural differences between the sexes, in order to have a theoretical basis for the demand for the social inequality of men and women. But while the new theory went deeper psychologically, its fine words about the dignity of woman, etc., merely served to maintain woman in her dependent position as man's servant.

I shall try to indicate later why and how a class society is so closely tied up with male rule over the family. But it should already be clear that any theory propounding the

universal significance of sex differences would appeal very
strongly to the champions of male, hierarchical class rule.
Herein lies one of the important reasons why Bachofen
won sympathy from the conservative camp. But it should
be pointed out that Bachofen himself largely overcame the
potential reactionary interpretation of his theory by exploring the principle of the differences between sexes in a radical way and by discovering earlier social and cultural
structures in which woman's superiority and authority
were evident.

One essential feature of the Romantic conception is that
the difference between the sexes is not viewed as something that is socially conditioned or had gradually developed in history; it was supposed to be a biological fact
that will never change. Relatively little effort has been
made to establish the real nature of masculine and feminine qualities. Some regarded the character of the bourgeois woman as an expression of her "essence." Others
pursued a superficial approach to difference between male
and female: Fichte, for example, believed that the whole
difference was based on their "natural" difference in behavior in the sex act.

The later Romantics equated "woman" with "mother,"
but they also turned away from vague conclusions and
began to undertake empirical investigations of the motherly principle in historical and biological reality. In so doing,
they added extraordinary depth to the mother-concept.
Especially Bachofen himself, although to some extent
sticking to the notion of the "naturalness" of the differences between the sexes, he also arrived at important new
insights. One was that woman's nature developed from her
real "practice" in life—her early care of the helpless
infant, necessitated by the biological situation.

This fact, along with several others already mentioned,
should suggest that Bachofen was hardly a full-fledged
romantic, as Klages and Bäumler would have us believe.
As we shall see, the "blessed" matriarchal society of
Bachofen contains many traits that reveal a close kinship
with the ideals of socialism. For example, concern for
man's material welfare and earthly happiness is presented
as one of the central ideas of matriarchal society. On
other points, too, the reality of matriarchal society as
described by Bachofen is closely akin to Socialist ideals

and goals and directly opposed to Romantic and reactionary aims. According to Bachofen, matriarchal society was
a primeval democracy where sexuality is free of Christian
depreciation, where maternal love and compassion are the
dominant moral principles, where injury to one's fellowman is the gravest sin, and where private property does
not yet exist. As Kelles-Krauz points out,[10] he characterizes matriarchal society by alluding to the old legend of
the sumptuous fruit tree and the miraculous spring: both
dried up when men converted them into private property.

Frequently, though by no means always, Bachofen re-
veals himself to be a dialectic thinker. Note this remark:
"In order to be comprehensible, the Demetrian gynecocracy demands the assumption of an earlier, cruder state of
affairs that would have been directly opposed to the basic
principles of the Demetrian way of life; the latter arose in
a struggle against this earlier situation. Thus the historical
reality of matriarchy is a testimony of the historical reality
of hetaerism."[11] Bachofen's philosophy is akin to that of
Hegel in many respects:

> The advance from the maternal conception of mankind to a
> paternal conception was the most important turning point
> in the history of the relationship between the sexes . . . In
> the accentuation of paternity we have the deliverance of
> the human spirit from the phenomena of nature; in the
> successful implementation of paternity we have the elevation
> of human existence above the laws of corporeal life.[12]

For Bachofen, the supreme goal of man's destiny is "the
elevation of earthly existence to the purity of the divine
father-principle."[13] He sees the victory of the paternal-
spiritual principle over the maternal-material principle realized historically in the victory of Rome over the Orient—
particularly over Carthage and Jerusalem:

> It was a Roman thought that spurred Europeans to put their
> stamp on the whole earth. The thought was simply this: that

[10] Kelles-Krauz, *Neue Zeit*, 1901–1902, I 522.
[11] J. J. Bachofen, *Der Mythus von Orient und Okzident, op. cit.*, p. 31.
[12] *Ibid.*, pp. 48–49.
[13] *Ibid.*, p. 57.

only the free rule of the spirit, not any physical law, determines the fate of peoples.[14]

There is obviously a sharp contradiction between the Bachofen who admires gynocratic democracy and the aristocratic Bachofen of Basel who opposed the political emancipation of woman and who said: "By force of circumstances, democracy always paves the way for tyranny; my ideal is a republic ruled, not by the many, but by the best citizens."[15] It is a contradiction that crops up on several different planes. On the philosophical plane, it is the believing Protestant and Idealist over against the Romantic; and the dialectic philosopher over against the naturalistic metaphysician. On the social and political plane, it is the anti-Democrat over against the admirer of a Communist-democratic social structure. On the moral plane, it is the proponent of Protestant-bourgeois morality over against the advocate of a society where sexual freedom reigned instead of monogamous marriage.

Unlike Klages and Bäumler, Bachofen makes no effort to harmonize these contradictions. The fact that he lets them stand is one reason why he won such wide approval from those Socialists who sought, not reform, but a thoroughgoing change of society's social and psychic structure.

The fact that Bachofen embodied such contradictions and scarcely tried to hide them is essentially due to the psychological and economic conditions of his personal existence. The breadth of his human and intellectual range is considerable, but his predilection for matriarchy apparently stemmed from his intense fixation on his own mother: he did not marry until he was forty, after the death of his mother. Moreover, his inheritance of ten million dollars permitted him to remain aloof from certain bourgeois ideals, and such aloofness was a necessity for any admirer of matriarchy. On the other hand, this patrician of Basel was so thoroughly rooted in his entrenched patriarchal tradition that he could not help but remain loyal to the traditional Protestant-bourgeois ideals. Neo-Romantics, such as Schuler, Klages, and Bäumler, saw only the Bachofen who propounded irrationalism, surrender to nature, and the exclusive rule of naturalist values based on

14 *Ibid.*, p. 571.
15 Kelles-Krauz, *op. cit.*, p. 522.

the blood bond and earthly ties. They solved the problem
of Bachofen's contradictions by adopting a one-sided interpretation of him.[16]

The Socialists, too, recognized the "mystic" side of
Bachofen, but they directed their attention and sympathy
to Bachofen the ethnologist and psychologist—i.e., to that
part of his work that accounts for his importance in the
history of scholarship.

It was Friedrich Engels, more than anyone else, who
made Bachofen's work known in the nineteenth century.
In his *Origin of the Family, Private Property, and the
State*, Engels asserts that the history of the family dates
from Bachofen's mother right. Naturally, he criticizes
Bachofen's Idealist position, which derives social relationships from religion, but says:

> None of this, however, detracts from his ground-breaking
> work. He was the first to replace an unknown primeval state

[16] Klages, who regards rational thought (*Geist*) as the destroyer of
"soul" handles the problem by regarding Bachofen's naturalistic metaphysics as the essential kernel of his thought, and viewing Bachofen's
Protestant idealism as secondary and incidental. Bäumler, who attacks
Klages's interpretation, truncates Bachofen's thought even more severely.
While Klages at least sees the anti-Protestant and anti-Idealist Bachofen,
Bäumler argues from his basically patricentric outlook and regards as incidental the most important part of Bachofen's work: his historical and
psychological statements about matriarchal society. He sees importance
only in Bachofen's naturalist metaphysics, and dismisses the depiction of
woman as the center and connecting link of the most ancient civil organization as a false assumption. To Bäumler it is also very doubtful that
monogamy should not be found at the very start of human history. For
him, matriarchy as a social reality is quite incidental:

> Chthonic religion continues to be of decisive importance for an
> understanding of primitive and pre-history, even if it turns out that
> there never was any Indo-European matriarchy. Bachofen's explana-
> tion is wholly independent of ethnological and linguistic findings in
> its most basic aspects, for the bases of his explanation do not rest
> upon hypotheses of a sociological or historical nature . . . The
> bases of Bachofen's philosophy of history lie in his metaphysics. The
> profundity of this metaphysics is the main point. His errors in the
> area of the philosophy of culture [i.e., his sociological and historical
> errors] are easily set right. A scholarly work on the beginnings of the
> human race, which was totally free of error, would leave nothing to
> be corrected; but it would provide nothing worth noticing either.
> (J. J. Bachofen, *Der Mythos von Orient und Okzident, op. cit.*, p.
> cclxxx.)

Bachofen "went too far" with his theory when he attributed to woman
the first advance of the human race. This, notes Bäumler, is a "false
hypothesis." The important thing is not the mother as a real, socially
and psychologically important phenomenon, but the religious category of
"mother," with which Bachofen has enriched the conscious awareness of
mankind and the philosophy of history in particular. We are not sur-
prised when Bäumler condemns as typically "Oriental" the affirmation
and approval of sexuality, which Bachofen regards as an essential trait
of matriarchy, and when he explains Bachofen's openness to sexual matters in such terms as his own personal "purity."

with a state of sexual intercourse unbound by rules. He did
this by pointing out that ancient classical literature gives us
many indications that monogamy was preceded by a prior
state among the Greeks and Asians. In this prior state, not
only did men have sexual relations with more than one
woman, but women also had sexual relations with more than
one man, without infringing against the mores. Furthermore,
he has shown us that the line of descent originally was traced
only through the female line, from mother to mother, and
that the exclusive validity of the female line of descent
continued for a long time—even into the eras of monogamy
when the knowledge of paternity was well established. This
original position of the mother, in which she was the only
sure parent of the child, ensured to mothers (and hence to
women) a higher social status than they have ever had since
then. Bachofen, to be sure, does not spell out these theses
so explicitly, because his mystical outlook prevented him
from doing so. But he did establish them, and this was a
revolutionary step in 1861.

Sixteen years later the American ethnologist, Lewis H.
Morgan, demonstrated the existence of a matriarchal social structure in a very different area; and he used methods that were quite different from those of Bachofen. His
book, *Ancient Society*, was thoroughly studied by Marx
and Engels, and served as the basis for Engels' work on
the family. Commenting on the matriarchal *gens* discovered by Morgan, Engels remarked that it had "the same
significance for prehistory that Darwin's theory of evolution had for biology and that Marx's theory of surplus
work had for political economy." There could be no
higher praise from Engels, who went on to say: "The
matriarchal *gens* has become the central point around
which the whole science turns. We now know where to
look, what to look for, and how to organize and group
our findings."

It was not only Engels who was impressed by the
discovery of matriarchy. Marx left behind a whole series
of critical notes, which Engels utilized in his work. Bebel
grounded his socialist best-seller, *Die Frau und der Sozialismus* (Woman and Socialism), on the theory of matriarchate. Similarly, Marx's son-in-law, Paul Lafargue, wrote
about the "awesome role of priestess and guardian of the

mysteries that woman had in the primitive communi-
ty"[17] and her attaining this role again in a future
society. Kelles-Krauz asserted that Bachofen dug under
the bourgeois renaissance and unearthed the precious
seeds of a new revolutionary renaissance: the renaissance
of the Communist spirit.[18]

What accounts for the Socialists' favorable attitude
toward the matriarchal theory? The first thing, as we
noted earlier in connection with the Romantics, was their
emotional and ideological distance from bourgeois society.
Bachofen had pointed out the relativity of existing societal
relationships. He had underlined the fact that monogamous marriage was not an eternal "natural" institution at
all. Such a view could only be welcomed by a theory and
political activity that advocated a fundamental change of
the existing social structure. In Bachofen's own political
position, this was a problematic aspect of his theory:

> The exclusivity of the marital bond seems so indispensable,
> so intimately tied up with the nobility of human nature and
> its lofty vocation, that most people regard it as the original
> state of affairs. The assertion that there were deeper, un-
> fettered relations between the sexes is regarded as a dismally
> erroneous or useless speculation on the beginnings of human
> existence; so it is sluffed off as a bad dream. Who wouldn't
> like to adopt the common view, to spare our species from
> the painful memory of its shameful early days? But the
> evidence of history prevents us from giving in to the prompt-
> ings of pride and egotism, from doubting the painfully slow
> progress of man towards higher marital morality.[19]

Aside from the fact that the theory of matriarchy
underlined the relativity of the bourgeois social structure,
its very special content could not but win the sympathy of
Marxists. First of all, it had discovered a period when
woman had been the authority and focal point of society,
rather than the slave of man and an object for barter; this
lent important support to the struggle for woman's political and social emancipation. The great battle of the
eighteenth century had to be picked up afresh by those
who were fighting for a classless society.

[17] Cited by Kelles-Krauz, op. cit., p. 6.
[18] Ibid., p. 524.
[19] J. J. Bachofen, Der Mythos von Orient und Okzident, op. cit., p. 30.

In terms of its psycho-social foundations, the patriarchal social structure is closely bound up with the class character of present-day society. This society is based, to an important degree, on specific psychic attitudes that are partially rooted in unconscious drives; and these psychic attitudes effectively complement the external coerciveness of the governmental apparatus. The patriarchal family is one of the most important loci for producing the psychic attitudes that operate to maintain the stability of class society.[20]

Let me focus on the most important aspect. We are dealing here with an emotional complex that might well be called the "patricentric" complex. Characteristically, it includes the following elements: affective dependence on fatherly authority, involving a mixture of anxiety, love and hate; identification with paternal authority vis-à-vis weaker ones; a strong and strict superego whose principle is that duty is more important than happiness; guilt feelings, reproduced over and over again by the discrepancy between the demands of the superego and those of reality, whose effect is to keep people docile to authority. It is this psycho-social condition that explains why the family is almost universally regarded as the foundation (or at least one of the important supports) of society; it also explains why any theoretical assault on the family, such as Bachofen's theory, would necessarily win the support of Socialist writers.

Of particular importance for our problem is the picture which Bachofen as well as Morgan give of the social, psychic, moral, and political relationships characteristic of matriarchy. But while Bachofen looks back nostalgically toward this earlier societal stage and regards it as having gone forever, Morgan talks about a higher stage of civilization that is yet to come: "It will be a recurrence, but on a higher level, of the freedom, equality and brotherhood characteristic of the ancient *gens*." Bachofen himself graphically describes these traits of freedom, equality, and brotherhood that were to be found in matriarchal society, whose governing principles are not anxiety and submissiveness, but love and compassion:[21]

[20] See Chapter 8.
[21] The relationship which stands at the origin of all culture, of every virtue, of every nobler aspect of existence, is that between mother and child; it operates in a world of violence as the divine principle of love,

Bachofen's favorable reception among socialists was also helped by the decisive role of concern for man's material happiness on earth played in matriarchal society. Although on the theoretical level, this naturalistic materialism, rooted in the mother's energy dedication to the betterment of man's natural life, is basically different from dialectic materialism, nevertheless it contains an acceptable social hedonism that explains why it was so well received by the proponents of socialism.

Some general remarks seem to be in order concerning the principle of a complete lack of sexual restrictions, which Bachofen attributes to early gynocratic society. It would certainly be erroneous to maintain that restrictions in the sexual sphere are to be explained purely in terms of the existence and nature of class society, and that a classless society would necessarily restore the unlimited sexual relations described by Bachofen. On the other hand, we must say that a morality which deprecates and devalues sexual pleasure does perform an important role in maintaining a class society and that any attack on this morality, such as Bachofen's theory certainly was, would

---

of union, of peace. Raising her young, the woman learns earlier than the man to extend her loving care beyond the limits of the ego to another creature, and to direct whatever gift of invention she possesses to the preservation and improvement of this other's existence. Woman at this stage is the repository of all culture, of all benevolence, of all devotion, of all concern for the living and grief for the dead. Yet the love that arises from motherhood is not only more intense, but also more universal. . . . Whereas the paternal principle is inherently restrictive, the maternal principle is universal; the paternal principle implies limitation to definite groups, but the maternal principle, like the life of nature, knows no barriers. The idea of motherhood produces a sense of universal fraternity among all men, which dies with the development of paternity. The family based on father right is a closed individual organism, whereas the matriarchal family bears the typically universal character that stands at the beginning of all development and distinguishes material life from higher spiritual life. Every woman's womb, the mortal image of the earth mother Demeter, will give brothers and sisters to the children of every other woman; the homeland will know only brothers and sisters until the day when the development of the paternal system dissolves the undifferentiated unity of the mass and introduces a principle of articulation.

The matriarchal cultures present many expressions and even juridical formulations of this aspect of the maternal principle. It is the basis of the universal freedom and equality so frequent among matriarchal peoples, of their hospitality, and of their aversion to restrictions of all sorts. . . . And in it is rooted the admirable sense of kinship and συμπάθεια (fellow feeling) which knows no barriers or dividing lines and embraces all members of a nation alike. Matriarchal states were particularly famed for their freedom from intestine strife and conflict. . . . The matriarchal peoples—and this is no less characteristic—assigned special culpability to the physical injury of one's fellow men or even of animals. . . . An air of tender humanity, discernible even in the facial expression of Egyptian statuary, permeates the culture of the matriarchal world. (J. J. Bachofen, *Myth, Religion, and Mother Right, op. cit.*, pp. 79–81.)

be a further reason for his favorable reception among the Socialists.

Sexuality offers one of the most elementary and powerful opportunities for satisfaction and happiness. If it were permitted to the full extent required for the productive development of the human personality, rather than limited by the need to maintain control over the masses, the fulfillment of this important opportunity for happiness would necessarily lead to intensified demands for satisfaction and happiness in other areas of life. Since the satisfaction of these further demands would have to be achieved through material means, these demands of themselves would lead to the breakup of the existing social order. Closely allied to this is another social function of restrictions on sexual satisfaction. Insofar as sexual pleasure as such is declared to be something sinful, while sexual desires remain perpetually operative in every human being, moral prohibitions always become a source of production for guilt feelings, which are often unconscious, or transferred to different matters.

These guilt feelings are of great social importance. They account for the fact that suffering is experienced as just punishment for one's own guilt, rather than blamed on the defects of the social organization. They eventually cause emotional intimidation, limiting people's intellectual—and especially their critical—capacities, while developing an emotional attachment to the representatives of social morality.

Let me add one final pertinent viewpoint. The clinical investigations and psychoanalytic individual psychology have been able to give us some indications that the suppression or acceptance of sexual satisfaction has important consequences for man's drives and character structure.[22] The development of the "genital character" is conditioned by the absence of sexual restraints, which impede the optimal development of a person. Among the qualities undoubtedly belonging to the genital character is psychic and intellectual independence, whose social relevance needs no further emphasis. On the other hand, the suppression of genital sexuality leads to the development or intensification of such instinctual tendencies as the anal, the sadistic and the latent homosexual, which are of deci-

[22] See Chapter 8.

sive importance for the instinctual basis of present-day society.

Whatever the present status of matriarchy research, however, it seems certain that there are societal structures which can be called matricentric. And if we are to understand the social structures of the present day and their transformations, attention should be given to the present and future findings of this research.

The libidinal strivings of human beings are among the social "productive forces" in society. By virtue of their flexibility and changeability, they can adapt themselves considerably to the existing economic and social situation of the group—though there are limits to this adaptability. The psychic structure shared by the members of a social group represents an indispensable support for the maintenance of social stability. This structure, of course, is a support for stability only so long as the contradictions between the psychic structure and economic conditions do not go beyond a certain threshold; if this threshold is passed, the psychic forces tend to change or dissolve the existing order; it is important, though, to remember that the psychic structures of different classes can be radically different or even opposed to each other, depending on their function in the social process.

Although the individual is psychically different from the members of his own group, because of his individual constitution and personal life experiences—particularly those of early childhood—a large sector of his psychic structure is the product of adaptation to the situation of his class and the whole society in which he lives. Our knowledge about the factors determining the psychic structure of a given class or society, and hence about the psychic "productive forces" that are operative in a given society, is far less advanced than our knowledge about economic and social structures. One of the reasons for this is that the student of these problems is himself molded by the psychic structure typical for his society; accordingly, he comprehends only that which is like him. He easily makes the mistake of regarding his own psychic structure, or that of his society, as "human nature." He can readily overlook the fact that, under different social conditions, quite different drive structures have been and can be operative as productive forces.

The study of "matricentric" cultures is important for the social sciences. Because it brings to light psychic structures that are wholly different from those observed in our society; at the same time, it throws new light on the "patricentric" principle.

The patricentric complex is a psychic structure in which one's relationship to the father (or his psychological equivalents) is the central relationship. In his concept of the (positive) Oedipus complex, Freud uncovered one of the decisive features of this structure—although he overestimated its universality because he lacked the necessary distance from his own society. The sexual impulses of the male infant, which are directed to his mother as the first and most important female "love-object," cause him to regard his father as a rival. This constellation acquires its characteristic significance from the further fact that in the patriarchal family the father simultaneously functions as the authority who governs the child's life. Quite apart from the physiological impossibility of the fulfillment of the child's wishes, the father's dual role has another affect that Freud pointed out: the child's desire to take the place of his father leads him to identify with his father to some degree. The child introjects the father, insofar as the latter is the representative of moral dictates, and this introjection is a powerful source for the formation of conscience. But since this process is only partially successful, the child's rivalry with the father leads to the development of an ambivalent emotional attitude. On the one hand, the child wants to be loved by his father; on the other hand, he more or less openly rebels against him.

However, the patricentric complex is also shaped by the psychic processes going on in the father himself. For one thing, he is jealous of his son. This is partly due to the fact that his lifeline is on the wane by comparison with that of his son. But an even more important cause of this jealousy is socially conditioned: it stems from the fact that the child's life situation is relatively free of social obligations. It is clear that this jealousy is greater where the weight of paternal responsibilities is heavier.

Still more important in determining the father's attitude toward his son are social and economic factors. Depending on economic circumstances, the son is either the heir to his father's estate or the future provider for his father in sickness and old age. He represents a sort of capital investment. From an economic viewpoint, the sums invested in his education and professional training are quite akin to those contributed toward accident insurance and old-age pensions.

Moreover, the son plays an important role insofar as the father's social prestige is concerned. His contributions to society and the concomitant social recognition can increase his father's prestige; his social failure can diminish or even destroy his father's prestige. (An economically or socially successful marriage by the son plays an equivalent role.)

Because of the son's social and economic function, the goal of his education is ordinarily not his personal happiness—i.e., the maximum development of his own personality; it is rather his maximum usefulness in contributing to the father's economic or social needs. Frequently, therefore, we find an objective conflict between the son's happiness and his usefulness; but this conflict is usually not consciously noticed by the father, since the ideology of his society leads him to see both goals as identical. The situation is further complicated by the fact that the father frequently identifies himself with his son: he expects his son not only to be socially useful, but also to fulfill his own unsatisfied wishes and fantasies.

These social functions of the son play a decisive role in the quality of the father's love: he loves his son on the condition that the son fulfill the expectations that are centered around him. If this is not the case, the father's love can end, or even turn to disdain or hate.[23]

The conditional nature of paternal love typically leads to two results: (1) loss of the psychic security that comes from the knowledge that one is loved unconditionally; (2) intensification of the role of conscience—i.e., the person develops an outlook in which the fulfillment of duty becomes the central concern of life, because only that can provide some minimum guarantee of being loved. But even maximal fulfillment of the demands of conscience

---

[23] This also accounts for the fact that the "favorite son"—the one who best fulfills his father's expectations—is a characteristic phenomenon in a patricentric culture.

will not prevent guilt feelings from arising, because the person's performance will always fall short of the ideals set before him.

By contrast, a mother's love for the child is typically[24] of a wholly different character. This is due, first and foremost, to the fact that it is completely unconditional in the first few years of life. Mother's care of the helpless infant is not dependent on any moral or social obligations to be carried out by the child; there is not even an obligation to return her love. The unconditional nature of motherly love is a biological necessity which may also foster a propensity for unconditional love in the woman's emotional disposition. The certainty that mother's (or her psychological equivalent's) love is not dependent on any conditions means that the fulfillment of moral dictates plays a much smaller role, since it is not the condition for being loved.

The traits just described differ sharply from the image of the mother that is cherished in present-day patricentric society. Basically, this society only knows about courage and heroism on the part of the man (in whom these qualities are really tinged with a large dose of narcissism). The image of the mother, on the other hand, has been a distorted one of sentimentality and weakness. In place of unconditional motherly love, which embraces not only one's own children but all children and all human beings, we find the specifically bourgeois sentiment of possessiveness injected into the mother image.

This change in the mother image represents a socially conditioned distortion of the mother-child relationship. A further consequence of this distortion—and also an expression of the Oedipus complex—is the attitude in which the desire to be loved by the mother is replaced by the desire to protect her and place her on a pedestal. No longer does the mother have the function of protecting; now she is to be protected and kept "pure." This reaction formation (distorting the original relationship to one's mother) is also extended to other mother symbols, such as country, nation, and the soil; and it plays an important role in the extremely patricentric ideologies of the present

---

[24] Obviously, I am talking here about paternal or maternal love in an ideal sense. The love of a particular father or mother will fall far short of this ideal presentation—for a wide variety of reasons.

day. Mother and her psychological equivalents have not disappeared in these ideologies, but they have changed their function from protecting figures to figures in need of protection.

Summing up, we can say that the patricentric individual—and society—is characterized by a complex of traits in which the following are predominant: a strict superego, guilt feelings, docile love for paternal authority, desire and pleasure at dominating weaker people, acceptance of suffering as a punishment for one's own guilt, and a damaged capacity for happiness. The matricentric complex, by contrast, is characterized by a feeling of optimistic trust in mother's unconditional love, far fewer guilt feelings, a far weaker superego, and a greater capacity for pleasure and happiness. Along with these traits there also develops the ideal of motherly compassion and love for the weak and others in need of help.[25]

While both types may well be found in any given society—depending primarily on the child's family constellation—it does seem that, as an average type, each is characteristic for a particular type of society. The patricentric type is probably dominant in bourgeois-Protestant society, while the matricentric type would play a relatively major role in the Middle Ages and in southern

[25] The patricentric type is related to the "anal character" and the "compulsive character" in psychoanalytic terminology, while the matricentric type is related to the "oral character." However, the latter is wholly different from the "oral-sadistic" character type. The oral-sadistic person, who has a parasitic quality wants only to take and is unwilling to give. He reacts with rage when his wishes are denied, not with grief as the matricentric type does.

However, there is a basic difference between the typology based on pregenital character structures and the matricentric and patricentric typology. The former signifies a pregenital fixation to the oral or anal level, and it is basically opposed to the mature, "genital character." The latter conceived in terms of the dominant object relationship, does not stand in basic opposition to the genital character. The matricentric type *can be* an oral character; in that case the person is more or less passive, dependent and in need of other's help. But the matricentric type can also be a "genital" character: i.e., phychically mature, active, not neurotic or arrested.

The typology chosen here disregards the question of the degree of maturity, and focuses on one aspect of the contents of the character structure. A complete presentation would, of course, have to deal with the differences between genital and pregenital character within both the matricentric and the patricentric type respectively. Here we cannot enter into a full discussion of the various psychoanalytic categories (see W. Reich, *Charakteranalyse*, Vienna, 1933). I do believe, however, that a typology based on object-relationships, rather than on "erogenous zones" or on clinical symptomatology, offers fruitful possibilities for social research. Also, we cannot discuss here the interesting problem of the relationship between our suggested types and Kretschmer's schizothymic and cyclothymic, Jaensch's integrated and disintegrated, and Jung's introverted and extroverted.

European society today. This leads us to Weber's treatment of the connection between bourgeois capitalism and the Protestant work ethos, in contrast to the connection between Catholicism and the work ethos of Catholic countries.

Whatever objections may be raised against specific theses of Weber, the fact of such a connection is now an assured part of scholarly knowledge. Weber himself treated the problem on the conscious and ideological level. But a complete understanding of the interrelationship can only be achieved by an analysis of the drive that serves as the basis for bourgeois-capitalism and the Protestant spirit.

While Catholicism also exhibits many patricentric traits—God the Father, hierarchy of male priests, etc.—the important role of the matricentric complex in it cannot be denied. The Virgin Mary and the Church herself psychologically represent the great Mother who shelters all her children in her bosom. Indeed, certain maternal traits are ascribed to God himself—though not in a conscious way. The individual "son of the Church" can be sure of Mother Church's love, so long as he remains her child or returns to her bosom. This child relationship is effected sacramentally. To be sure, moral dictates play a major role. But a complicated mechanism operates to insure that these dictates retain their necessary social weight while, at the same time, the individual believer can have the certainty of being loved without reference to the moral sphere. Catholicism produces guilt feelings in no small measure; at the same time, however, it provides the means for freeing oneself from these feelings. The price one must pay is affective attachment to the Church and her servants.

Protestantism, on the other hand, has done a thorough job of expurgating the matricentric traits of Christianity. Mother substitutes, such as the Virgin Mary or the Church, have disappeared, as have maternal traits in God. At the center of Luther's[26] theology we find doubt or

---

[26] Psychologically speaking, Luther was an extremely patricentric type. An ambivalent attitude toward the father pervades his life. It manifests itself in the fact that he always focused on two father figures at the same time: one whom he loves, the other one whom he hates and disdains. He has no understanding at all for the notion of enjoying life, or for a culture in which such pleasure plays a central role; thus he himself is one of the great haters. He is related to the compulsive-neurotic, homosexual type; but that does not mean to say that he himself was a compulsive-neurotic or a homosexual in the clinical sense.

despair that sinful man can have any certainty of being loved. And there is only one remedy: faith.[27] In Calvinism and many other Protestant sects, this remedy proves to be insufficient. It is complemented in a decisive way by the role assigned to the fulfillment of one's duty ("innerworldly asceticism"), and by the necessity for "success" in secular life as the only proof of God's favor and grace.[28]

The rise of Protestantism is conditioned by the same social and economic factors that made possible the rise of the "spirit" of capitalism. And, like every religion, Protestantism has the function of continually reproducing and strengthening the drive structure that is necessary for a particular society. The patricentric complex—in which fulfillment of duty and success are the major driving forces of life, while pleasure and happiness play a secondary role—represents one of the most powerful productive forces behind the enormous economic and cultural efforts of capitalism. Until the capitalist era, people (e.g., slaves) had to be compelled by physical force to dedicate every ounce of energy to economically useful work. Through the influence of the patricentric complex, people began to show the same total dedication of their own "free will," because the external compunction was now internalized. The internalization was effected most completely among the ruling classes of bourgeois society, who were the authentic representatives of the specifically bourgeois work ethos. In contrast to external force, however, the internali-

[27] The full significance of the thesis "justification through faith alone" can only be explained in terms of compulsive-neurotic thought mechanisms and their accompanying doubts. We cannot go into greater detail here.

Today I would make a significant addition to this interpretation. Precisely because of Luther's ambivalence (to the father figure, hate against his father and the authorities of the Catholic Church, and friendliness toward the secular princes, accompanied by hate against the rebellious peasants) he yearned for the unconditional love from mother. Only in it could he feel the security of being loved.

[28] In terms of our present problems, the Jewish religion has quite a complicated character. It clearly bears the stamp of a reaction against the matricentric religions of the Near East. Its concept of God, like that of Protestantism, contains only fatherly-male traits.

On the other hand, the image of the great mother has not been wiped out; it is retained in the notion of the holy land, flowing "with milk and honey." Here the decisive thought of the Jewish religion is this: We have sinned, and God has driven us out of our land as a punishment; but he will return us to that land when we have suffered enough. This land, visualized in the Prophetic literature as one which has all the qualities of the fertile, never frustrating soil, has taken on the role of the Great Mother of matriarchal religions.

In the Messianic concept and the faith in the return to the Holy Land (characterized by painless childbirth, and the cessation of the necessity of work), the idea of an unconditionally loving mother was preserved.

zation process led to a different result: Fulfilling the dictates of conscience offered a satisfaction that contributed greatly to the solidification of the patricentric structure.[29]

This satisfaction, however, was quite limited, because fulfillment of duty and economic success were poor substitutes for traits now lost: the capacity to enjoy life, and the inner security derived from knowing that one is loved unconditionally. Moreover, the spirit of *homo homini lupus* led to personal isolation and an incapacity for love—a heavy psychic burden on the psyche, which tended to undermine the patricentric structure, even though the decisive factors operating to undermine the structure were rooted in economic changes.

While patricentric structure had been the psychic driving force behind the economic achievements of bourgeois-Protestant society, at the same time it produced the conditions that would destroy the patricentric structure and lead to a renaissance of a matricentric one. The growth of man's productive capacity made it possible, for the first time in history, to visualize the realization of a social order that previously had only found expression in fairy tales and myths, an order where all men would be provided with the material means necessary for their real happiness, with relatively little expenditure of individual effort in actual labor, where men's energies would be expended primarily in developing their human potential rather than in creating the economic goods that are absolutely necessary for the existence of a civilization.

The most progressive philosophers of the French enlightenment outgrew the emotional and ideological complex of the patricentric structure. But the real, full-fledged representative of the new matricentric tendencies proved to be the class whose motive for total dedication to work was prompted basically by economic considerations rather than by an internalized compunction: the working class. This same emotional structure provided one of the conditions for the effective influence of Marxist socialism on the

---

[29] When I talk about work and work ethos here, I am referring to a specific, concrete historical phenomenon: the bourgeois notion of work. Work certainly has many other psychic functions that are not considered here. It is an expression of social responsibility and a chance for creative activity. There is a work ethos in which these aspects are the dominant ones.

working class—insofar as its influence depended on the specific nature of their drive structure.

The psychic basis[30] of the Marxist social program was predominantly the matricentric complex. Marxism is the idea that if the productive capabilities of the economy were organized rationally, every person would be provided with a sufficient supply of the goods he needed—no matter what his role in the production process was; furthermore, all this could be done with far less work on the part of each individual than had been necessary up to now, and finally, every human being has an unconditional right to happiness in life, and this happiness basically resides in the "harmonious unfolding of one's personality"—all these ideas were the rational, scientific expression of ideas that could only be expressed in fantasy under earlier economic conditions: Mother Earth gives all her children what they need, without regard for their merits.

It is this connection between matricentric tendencies and Socialist ideas that explains why the "materialist-democratic" character of matriarchal societies led Socialist authors to express such warm sympathy for the theory of matriarchy.

---

[30] It should be obvious that these psychological considerations deal only with psychic productive forces; they do not explain socialism as a psychological phenomenon, nor do they seek to replace rational discussion of its theories with a psychological interpretation.

8

THE METHOD AND FUNCTION
OF AN ANALYTIC SOCIAL PSYCHOLOGY

NOTES ON PSYCHOANALYSIS
AND HISTORICAL MATERIALISM

PSYCHOANALYSIS IS A materialistic psychology, which should be classed among the natural sciences. It points to instinctual drives and needs as the motive force behind human behavior, these drives being produced by physiologically based *instincts* that are not directly observable in themselves. Psychoanalysis has shown that man's conscious psychic activity is only a relatively small sector of his psychic life, that many decisive impulses behind psychic behavior are unconscious. In particular, it has unmasked individual and collective ideologies as the expression of specific wishes and needs rooted in the instincts and shown that our "moral" and idealistic motives are in some measure the disguised and rationalized expression of instinctual drives.

Quite in line with the popular division of instincts into those of hunger and love, Freud began by assuming that two groups, the instincts for self-preservation and the sexual instincts,[1] served as the real motive force behind

["The Method and Function of an Analytic Social Psychology" was first published in the *Zeitschrift für Sozialforschung*, Hirshfeld-Leipzig, 1932.]
[1] Impressed by the libidinal admixtures in the instincts for self-preservation and the special significance of the destructive tendencies, Freud has modified his original position. Over against the life-maintaining (erotic) instincts, he now sets the death instinct. Significant as Freud's argument is for this modification in his original position, it is far more speculative and less empirical than his original position. To me it seems to rest upon an intermingling of biological data and psychological tendencies, an intermingling that Freud has otherwise avoided. It also stands in contrast

man's psychic life. He labeled the energy inherent in the sexual instincts as libido, and the psychic processes deriving from this energy as libidinous.[2] With respect to the sexual instincts, Freud extended the ordinary use of this term and included under it all the urges which, like the genital impulses, are physically conditioned, attached to certain *erogenous zones* of the body, and seek for pleasurable tension-release.

Freud assumes that the chief principle of psychic activity is the "pleasure principle," that is, the urge to discharge instinctual tensions in a way that will bring the maximum amount of pleasure. This pleasure principle is modified by the "reality principle": taking reality into account may lead us to renounce or postpone pleasure in order to avoid a greater discomfort or to gain even greater pleasure at some future time.

Freud sees the specific instinctual structure of the individual conditioned by two factors: his inherited physical constitution and his life experiences—in particular, the experiences of early childhood. Freud proceeds on the assumption that man's inherited constitution and life experiences form a "complementary chain" and that the specific task of analysis is to explore and uncover the influence of life experiences on the inherited instinctual constitution. Thus the analytic method is exquisitely historical: *it seeks to understand the drive structure through the understanding of life history*. This method is valid for the psychic life of healthy people as well as for the sick and neurotic. What distinguishes the neurotic from the "normal" person is the fact that the latter has successfully adapted his instinctual structure to his real needs in life, while the former's instinctual structure has run up against

with an original viewpoint of Freud, which saw the instincts primarily as wishing, desiring, and serving man's strivings for life. One of the consequences of Freud's overall position, it seems to me, is that man's psychic activity develops as an adaptation to life's processes and necessities, and that the instincts as such are contrary to the biological death principle. Discussion about the hypothesis of death instincts is still going on within psychoanalysis. In our presentation here, we take off from Freud's original position.

[2] At the time of writing this paper I adhered to the Freudian libido theory and hence speak of "libidinal forces" (energies) or of "libidinal structure" (or drive structure) where today I would not refer to the "libido" but to passionate forces of various kinds. For the main points of this paper this difference, however, is not too relevant. (1970)

certain obstacles that hinder him from satisfactorily adapt-
ing it to reality.

In order to make as clear as possible that sex instincts
can be modified and adapted to reality, we must point out
certain characteristics which clearly distinguish them from
the instincts for self-preservation. For example, unlike the
instincts for self-preservation, the sex instincts are post-
ponable. The former are more imperative because if they
are left unsatisfied too long, death will ensue; in short,
prolonged postponement of their satisfaction is psychologically intolerable. This means that the instincts for self-
preservation have primacy over the sex instincts—not that
they play a greater role in themselves, but in case of
conflict they are more urgent.

In addition, the sex-rooted drives can be repressed,
while the desires emanating from the instincts for self-
preservation cannot simply be removed from consciousness and placed in the unconscious. Another important
distinction between the two groups of instincts is the fact
that the sexual instincts can be sublimated: in other
words, instead of being satisfied directly, a sexual wish can
be satisfied in a way that may be far removed from the
original sexual goal and blended with other ego accomplishments. The instincts for self-preservation are not capable of such sublimation. Furthermore, the drives toward
self-preservation must be satisfied by real, concrete means,
while the sex drives can often be satisfied by pure fantasies. A man's hunger can only be satisfied by food; his
desire to be loved, however, can be satisfied by fantasies
about a good and loving God, and his sadistic tendencies
can be satisfied by sadistic spectacles and phantasies.

A final important distinction is that the sex drives,
unlike the drives toward self-preservation, can find expression in ways that are highly interchangeable and replace-
able. If one instinctual drive is not satisfied, it can be
replaced by others whose satisfaction is possible for either
internal or external reasons. The interchangeability and
replaceability of the sex drives is one of the keys to
understanding both neurotic and healthy psychic life, and
it is a cornerstone of the psychoanalytic theory. But it is
also a social fact of the highest significance. It permits the
masses to be offered (and satisfied by) those precise

satisfactions that are socially available and desirable from the standpoint of the ruling classes.[3]

Summing up, it can be said that the sexual instincts, which can be postponed, repressed, sublimated, and interchanged, are much more elastic and flexible than the instincts for self-preservation. The former lean on the latter, and follow their lead.[4] The greater flexibility and changeability of the sex instincts does not mean, however, that they can be left unsatisfied permanently; there is not only a physical but also a psychic minimum existence, and the sex instincts must be satisfied to some minimal extent. The differences between the two groups of drives, as we have noted them here, suggests rather that the sex instincts can make great adaptations to the real possibilities for satisfaction that exist, that is, to the concrete conditions of life. They grow and develop through this adaptation, and only in neurotic individuals do we find disturbances in this capacity for adaptation. Psychoanalysis has specifically pointed to the modifiability of the sex drives. It has taught us to understand the individual's instinctual structure in terms of his life experiences, to see how the former has been influenced by the latter. *The active and passive adaptation of the biological apparatus, the instincts, to social reality* is the key conception of psychoanalysis, and every exploration into personal psychology proceeds from this conception.

In the very beginning—and even later on—Freud concerned himself with the psychology of the individual. But once the instincts were discovered to be the motive force behind human behavior, and once the unconscious was seen as the source of man's ideologies and behavior patterns, it was inevitable that analytic authors would make an attempt to move from the problem of the individual to the problem of society, from individual to social psychology. They had to try to use the techniques of psychoanalysis to discover the hidden sources of the obviously irrational behavior patterns in societal life—in religion, custom, politics, and education. This obviously meant that

[3] The stimulation and satisfaction of sadistic impulses plays a special role. These impulses grow when other instinctual satisfactions of a more positive nature are ruled out on socio-economic grounds. Sadism is the great instinctual reservoir, to which one appeals when one has no other—and usually more costly—satisfactions to offer the masses; at the same time, it is useful in annihilating the "enemy."

[4] See Sigmund Freud, *Three Essays on the Theory of Sexuality.*

they would encounter difficulties that were avoided so long as they restricted themselves to the realm of individual psychology.

But these difficulties do not alter the fact that the inquiry itself was a legitimate scientific consequence of the starting point of psychoanalysis. If instinctual life and the unconscious were the key to understanding human behavior, then psychoanalysis was also entitled and competent to say something about the motives underlying social behavior. For "society" too consists of living individuals, who must be subject to the same psychological laws that psychoanalysis discovered in the individual.

Thus it seems erroneous if one—as Wilhelm Reich, for example—restricts psychoanalysis to the sphere of individual psychology and to argue against its applicability to social phenomena (politics, class consciousness, etc.).[5] The fact that a phenomenon is studied in sociology certainly does not mean that it cannot be an object of psychoanalysis (no more than study of an object's physical characteristics rules out study of its chemical aspects). What is meant is simply that it is an object of psychoanalysis only and wholly insofar as psychic factors play a role in the phenomenon. The thesis that psychology only deals with the individual while sociology only deals with "society" is false. For just as psychology always deals with a socialized individual, so sociology always deals with a group of individuals whose psychic structure and mechanisms must be taken into account. Later we will discuss the role that psychic factors play in societal phenomena, and point to the function of *analytical social psychology*.

The theory of society with which psychoanalysis seems to have both the greatest affinity and also the greatest differences is *historical materialism*.

---

[5] "The real object of psychoanalysis is the psychic life of socialized man. The masses come in for consideration only insofar as individual-based phenomena crop up in them (e.g., the problem of the leader), and only insofar as traits of the 'mass psyche'—anxiety, panic, obedience, etc—can be clarified from our knowledge of individuals. It would seem that the phenomenon of class consciousness is hardly accessible to psychoanalysis, and that sociological problems (mass movements, politics, etc) cannot be the object of the psychoanalytic method" (Wilhelm Reich, "Dialektischer Materialismus und Psychoanalyse," *Unter dem Banner des Marxismus*, III, 5, p. 737).
Because of the theoretical importance of this methodological problem, I stress my difference with the standpoint of Reich just presented; in his latest works Reich seems to have modified this standpoint in a very fruitful way. Later on I shall refer to my many points of agreement with his outstanding empirical investigations into social psychology.

They seem to have the most points of contact because they both are materialistic sciences. They do not start from "ideas" but from earthly life and needs. They are particularly close in their appraisal of consciousness, which is seen by both as less the driving force behind human behavior than the reflection of other hidden forces. But when it comes to the nature of the factors that truly condition man's consciousness, there seems to be an irreconcilable opposition between the two theories. Historical materialism sees consciousness as the expression of social existence; psychoanalysis sees it as determined by instinctual drive. Certain questions are unavoidable: do the two views contradict each other? If not, how are they related? Can the use of the psychoanalytic method enrich historical materialism? If so, how?

Before we discuss these questions, however, it seems necessary to examine the presuppositions that psychoanalysis brings to a study of societal problems.[6] Freud never assumed isolated man, devoid of all social ties, to be the object of psychology.

> Individual psychology, to be sure, is concerned with the individual human being, and it examines the ways in which he tries to satisfy his instinctual drives. But only rarely and under specific exceptional circumstances is it in a position to abstract from this person's relationships with other individuals. In the individual's psychic life, other people ordinarily must be considered as either models, objects, helpers or opponents. Thus, from the beginning, individual psychology is simultaneously social psychology—in this extended but legitimate sense.[7]

On the other hand, Freud basically ruled out the illusion of a social psychology whose object is a group as such, "society," or a social complex with a "mass soul" or "societal soul." Rather, he always proceeds from the fact that every group is composed only of individuals and that only the individual as such is the subject of psychic properties. Freud likewise refused to accept the notion of a

[6] On the methodological aspect, see my extensive treatment in E. Fromm, *The Dogma of Christ, op. cit.,* also S. Bernfeld, "Sozialismus und Psychoanalyse mit Diskussionsbemerkungen von E. Simmel und B. Lantos," *Der Sozialistische Arzt,* II, 2–3, 1929; Reich *op. cit.*
[7] Sigmund Freud, *Group Psychology and the Analysis of the Ego.*

"social instinct." What people called the "social instinct," he felt, was "not a primitive, elemental instinct." He sees the "origins of its development in a narrower circle, such as the family." His views lead to the conclusion that the social attributes owe their origin, intensification, and diminution to the influence of specific living conditions and environmental relations on the instincts.

Just as, for Freud, it is always socialized man who is the object of psychology, so he sees man's environment and living conditions playing a decisive role in his psychic development and in our theoretical understanding of it. Freud recognized the biological and physiological influence of the instincts; but he specifically emphasized to what degree these instincts could be modified, and he pointed to the environment, social reality, as the modifying factor.

Thus psychoanalysis seems to include presuppositions that make its method useful for investigations in social psychology and that rule out any conflict with sociology. It seeks to know the psychic traits common to the members of a group, and to explain these common psychic traits in terms of shared life experiences. These life experiences, however, do not lie in the realm of the personal or the accidental—the larger the group is, the more this holds true—but rather they are identical with the socioeconomic situation of this particular group. *Thus analytical social psychology seeks to understand the instinctual apparatus of a group, its libidinous and largely unconscious behavior, in terms of its socio-economic structure.*

Here an objection seems to be in order. Psychoanalysis explains instinctual development in terms of the life experiences of the earliest childhood years: that is to say, in terms of a period when the human being scarcely has anything to do with "society" but lives almost exclusively in the circle of his family. How then, according to psychoanalytic theory, can socio-economic relationships acquire such significance?

There is no real problem here at all. Of course, the first critical influences on the growing child come from the family. But the family itself, all its typical internal emotional relationships and the educational ideals it embodies, are in turn conditioned by the social and class background of the family; in short, they are conditioned by the social structure in which it is rooted. (For example: the emotional relationships between father and son are quite different in the family that is part of a bourgeois, patriarchal society than they are in the family that is part of a matriarchal society.) The family is the medium through which the society or the social class stamps its specific structure on the child, and hence on the adult. *The family is the psychological agency of society.*

Up to now the vast majority of psychoanalytic works, which have tried to apply psychoanalysis to social problems, have not met the requirements incumbent on any analytical social psychology.[8] Their failure begins in their assessment of the family's function. They saw clearly enough that the individual can only be understood as a socialized being. They realized that it is the child's relationships with the various family members that have a decisive influence on his instinctual development. But they have almost completely overlooked the fact that the family itself, in its whole psychological and social structure, with all its specific educational goals and emotional attitudes, is the product of a specific social and (in a narrower sense) class structure; that it is in fact simply the psychological agency of the society and class from which it comes. They had found the correct starting point for explaining the psychological influence of society on the child, but failed to take notice of it.

How was that possible? The psychoanalytic investigators were simply duped by a prejudice that they shared with every bourgeois investigator—even those who were progressive. They had turned bourgeois, capitalist society into an absolute; and they more or less consciously believed that it was the "normal" society, that its conditions and psychic factors were typical for "society" in general.

But there was another special reason why the analytical authors fell into this error. The object of their investigations were, first and foremost, sick and healthy members of modern society and largely of the middle classes; in

---

[8] Leaving aside worthless investigations (e.g., A. Kolnai's superficial studies of psychoanalysis and sociology, and such works as *Psychoanalyse der europäischen Politik*), we would apply the same criticism to authors such as Reik and Roheim who have dealt with themes in social psychology. There are exceptions, however. S. Bernfeld has focused admirably on the social conditioning of all pedagogical efforts in *Sysiphos oder üched die Grenzen der Erziehung.* Another exception is Wilhelm Reich, whose evaluation of the role of the family is in broad agreement with the view developed in this paper. In particular, Reich had done extensive research into the social conditioning and the social function of sexual morality.

short, they were members of the bourgeois class,[9] with the same social background. What determined and differentiated their individual lives, then, were the individual, personal and from a social standpoint, accidental experiences above this generally shared foundation. All the persons studied shared the same psychic traits, insofar as these traits were the product of an authoritarian society organized around the facts of class structures and the methodical pursuit of maximal profit. They differed psychologically only insofar as one had an overly strict father who terrified him in childhood, another had an older sister who was the focus of all his love, and still another had such an overpossessive mother that he was never able to break his libidinal ties with her.

To be sure, these personal experiences were of the utmost importance for the development of the individual concerned. By removing the psychic problems that had arisen from these experiences, psychoanalysis did its full duty as a therapy; it transformed the patient into a human being who was now adjusted to the existing social order. The goal of therapy did not go beyond that, nor did it have to. Unfortunately, our theoretical understanding of the whole situation did not get beyond that, either. Neglect of the social structure, which conditioned the family structure, may have been a source of error; but it was irrelevant in actual practice for individual psychology. When it came to research in social psychology, however, what had once been an irrelevant mistake now became a disastrous source of error affecting the whole endeavor.[10]

Psychoanalysis had focused on the structure of bourgeois society and its patriarchal family as the normal situation. Following the approach of individual psycholo-

[9] Psychologically, we must distinguish in the individual the traits that are typical for the whole society from the traits that are typical of his class. *But since the psychic structure of the whole society is stamped on the individual classes in certain basic traits*, the specific class traits, for all their importance, are of secondary importance vis-à-vis those of the whole society. Indeed one of the characteristics of a class society, concealed by ideologies, is the opposition between the relative uniformity of the different classes' psychic structure and their conflicting economic interests. The more a society breaks down economically, socially, and psychologically, the more the dominating and binding force of the overall society or ruling class disappears, the greater become the differences in the psychic structure of the various classes.

[10] I no longer believe that it is only an "irrelevant error" not to understand the socially conditioned traits of the individual patient. On the contrary, without such understanding one misses essential factors in the character structure of the patient. (1970)

gy, it had learned to appreciate individual differences in terms of the fortuitous traumas that befell individual men. In the beginning psychoanalytic researchers explained the various phenomena of social psychology in a corresponding way: they viewed them in terms of traumas, of socially fortuitous events. This necessarily led to a renunciation of the authentic analytic method. Since they did not concern themselves with the variety of life experiences, the socio-economic structure of other types of society, and therefore did not try to explain their psychic structure as determined by their social structure, they necessarily began to *analogize* instead of *analyzing*. They treated mankind or a given society as an individual, transposed the specific mechanisms found in contemporary individuals to every possible type of society, and "explained" the psychic structure of these societies by analogy with certain phenomena (usually of a neurotic sort) typical of human beings in their own society.

In doing this, they overlooked a point of view that is fundamental even to psychoanalytic individual psychology. They forgot the fact that neurosis—whether a neurotic symptom or a neurotic character trait—results from the "abnormal" individual's faulty adaptation of his instinctual drives to the reality around him; most people in a society, i.e., the "healthy" people, do possess this ability to adapt. Thus phenomena studied in social (or mass) psychology cannot be explained by analogy with neurotic phenomena. They should be understood as the result of the adaptation of the instinctual apparatus to the social reality.

The most striking example of this procedure is the absolutization of the Oedipus complex, which was made into a universal human mechanism, even though sociological and ethnological studies indicated that this particular emotional relationship was probably typical only of families in a patriarchal society. The absolutizing of the Oedipus complex led Freud to base the whole development of mankind on the mechanism of father hatred and the resultant reactions,[11] without any regard for the material living conditions of the group under study.

Even when he started from a false sociological standpoint, however, a genius like Freud was able to make

---

[11] See Sigmund Freud, *Totem and Taboo.*

worthwhile and significant discoveries.[12] But in the work
of other analytical authors, this false starting point led to
results which compromised psychoanalysis in the eyes of
sociology, and of Marxist social theory in particular.

But the blame did not rest with psychoanalysis as such.
In fact, one only had to apply the classical method of
psychoanalytic individual psychology in a logical way to
social psychology, in order to arrive at results that would
meet with no objections. The fault was that psychoanalytic
authors did not utilize this method is a correct way when
they transferred it from the individual to social groups and
social phenomena.

Here a further clarification is called for. We have emphasized the modifiability of the instinctual apparatus
through the influence of external (and ultimately social)
factors. But one should not overlook the fact that the
instinctual apparatus, both quantitatively and qualitatively,
has certain physiologically and biologically determined
limits to its modifiability and that only within these limits
is it subject to the influence of social factors. Because of
the force of the energy it sends forth, moreover, the
instinctual apparatus itself is an extremely active force;
inherent in it is the tendency to alter living conditions so
that they serve instinctual goals.

In the interplay of interacting psychic drives and

[12] In the *Future of an Illusion* (1927), Freud softens this position that
neglects social reality and its changes. Recognizing the significance of
economic conditions, he moves from the standpoint of individual psychology and the question of how religion is psychologically possible for the
individual (a repetition of the child's attitude toward its father) to the
social psychological question why religion is socially possible and necessary. His answer is that religion was necessary so long as mankind needed
religious illusions to make up for their impotence (i.e., the low degree of
productive capability) vis-à-vis nature. With the growth of technology
and the concomitant maturation of mankind, religion became a superfluous and pernicious illusion.

This book of Freud does not consider all the socially relevant functions
of religion. In particular, it does not consider the important question of
the connection between specific forms of religion and specific social
constellations. But in method and content this work of Freud comes
closest to a materialistic social psychology. As far as content is concerned,
we need only cite this sentence from it: "It need hardly be pointed out
that a culture which leaves so many members unsatisfied and discontent
has little prospect of lasting long, and is doing little to achieve that goal."

Freud's book is in line with the standpoint of Marx as a young man,
who could use as his motto: "The abolition of religion, the illusory
happiness of the proletariat, is the demand to promote his true happiness.
The demand to give up illusions about his condition is the summons to
give up a condition which needs illusions. At its core, criticism of religion is criticism of the vale of tears whose halo is religion" ("Zur
Kritik der Hegelschen Rechtsphilosophie," *Lit. Nachlass*, I, [1923], 385).
In his latest work dealing with problems in social psychology, *Civilization
and Its Discontents*, Freud does not develop this line either in method or
in content. Rather, it should be regarded as an antithesis to the *Future of
an Illusion*.

economic conditions, the latter have primacy. Not in the sense that they represent the "stronger" motive; this question is spurious because we are not dealing with quantitatively comparable motives on the same plane. They have primacy in the sense that the satisfaction of the need for self-preservation is tied up with material production; and that the modifiability of the economic reality is more restricted than the modifiability of the human instinctual apparatus—in particular, the sexual instinct.

Applying the method of psychoanalytic individual psychology to social phenomena, we find that *the phenomena of social psychology are to be understood as processes involving the active and passive adaptation of the instinctual apparatus to the socio-economic situation. In certain fundamental respects, the instinctual apparatus itself is a biological given; but it is highly modifiable. The role of primary formative factors goes to the economic conditions. The family is the essential medium through which the economic situation exerts its formative influence on the individual's psyche. The task of social psychology is to explain the shared, socially relevant, psychic attitudes and ideologies—and their unconscious roots in particular—in terms of the influence of economic conditions on libido strivings.*

So far, then, the method of analytic social psychology seems to dovetail with the method of Freudian individual psychology and with the requirements of historical materialism. But new difficulties arise when this method is confused with an erroneous but widespread interpretation of the Marxist theory: the notion that historical materialism is a psychological theory or, more specifically, an economistic psychology.

If it were true, as Bertrand Russell claims,[13] that Marx

---

[13] In "Why Is Psychoanalysis Popular?" (*Forward*, 1927), Russell writes: "Of course psychoanalysis is incompatible with Marxism. For Marx stresses the economic motive which, at best, is tied up with self-preservation, while psychoanalysis stresses the biological motive which is tied up with self-preservation through reproduction. Clearly the two points of view are one-sided, since both motives play a role."

Russell then talks about a hypothetical mayfly, which would have only organs for eating in the larva stage and only organs for love-making in the adult stage. What would such an insect say, if it could think? Says Russell: "In the larva stage it would be a Marxist, in the adult stage a Freudian." Russell then adds that Marx, "the bookworm of the British Museum," is the representative of the larva's philosophy. Russell himself feels closer to Freud, since the latter "is not insensitive to the joys of love-making, and does not try to explain things in terms of 'making money,' that is, in terms of the orthodox economy created by desiccated old men."

saw "making money" and Freud saw "love" as the decisive
motive of human conduct, then the two theories would be
as irreconcilable as Russell believes. Consider his hypothetical example of the mayfly. Assuming that such a creature
could think theoretically, I do not think it would say what
Russell claims it would. Instead it would say that Russell
had completely misinterpreted both psychoanalysis and
Marxism; that psychoanalysis actually investigates the
adaptation of biological factors (the instincts) to social
reality, and that Marxism is not a psychological theory at
all.

Russell is not the only one to misconstrue the two
theories. He is joined by many other theoreticians, and his
false view is matched by many similar ones.

The notion of historical materialism being an economistic psychology is espoused by Hendrik de Man with special emphasis.

> As we know, Marx himself never formulated his theory of
> human motivation. As a matter of fact, he never explained
> what "class" meant. Death cut short his last work, when he
> was turning to this subject. But the basic conceptions from
> which he starts are not in doubt. Even undefined the tacit
> presupposition underlying his work appears both in his
> scholarly and political activity. Every economic thesis and
> every political opinion of Marx rests on the presupposition
> that man's volitional motives, which bring about social
> progress, are dictated first and foremost by economic in-
> terests. Present-day social psychology would express the same
> thoughts in terms of the effect of the acquisitive drive on
> social conduct. If Marx himself regarded such formulations
> as superfluous, that is because he took it for granted that this
> was the object and aim of contemporary political economy.[14]

Now this "tacit presupposition" may well have been the
self-understood conception of all contemporary (i.e.,
bourgeois) economists; but it certainly was not the view
of Marx himself, who did not share the views of contemporary theoreticians on many points.

Though in a less explicit way, Bernstein is not far from
this psychologistic interpretation when he tries to defend
the honor of historical materialism with this observation:

[14] Hendrik de Man, *Zur Psychologie des Sozialismus*, 1927, p. 281.

The economic interpretation of history need not mean that
only economic forces and motives are to be recognized, but
simply that economics is *always the decisive factor* that serves
as the cornerstone for the great movements of history.[15]

Behind these muddy formulations lies the notion that
Marxism is an economic psychology, which is purified and
improved by Bernstein in an idealist sense.[16]

The idea that the "acquisitive drive" is the basic or only
motive of human behavior is the brainchild of bourgeois
liberalism, used as a psychological argument against the
possibility of the realization of socialism.[17] Marx's petit-
bourgeois interpreters interpreted his theory as an
economistic psychology. In reality, historical materialism
is far from being a psychological theory; its psychological
presuppositions are few and may be briefly listed: *men*
make their own history; *needs* motivate men's actions and
feelings (hunger and love)[18]; these needs increase in the
course of historical development, thereby spurring increased economic activity.[19]

In connection with psychology, the economic factor
plays a role in historical materialism only to the extent
that human needs—primarily the need for self-
preservation—are largely satisfied through the production
of goods; in short, needs are the lever that stimulates
production. Marx and Engels certainly stressed that the
drive toward self-preservation took priority over all other
needs, but they did not go into any detail about the quality

[15] Bernstein, *Die Voraussetzungen des Sozialismus und die Aufgaben
der Sozialdemokratie*, Stuttgart, 1899, p. 13.
[16] At the very start of his book, *Der historische Materialismus*, Kautsky
firmly rejects the psychologistic interpretation. But he then goes on to
supplement historical materialism with a purely idealist psychology, by
assuming that there is a pristine "social drive."
[17] Indeed, many of the objections raised against historical materialism
actually apply to the specifically bourgeois admixtures smuggled into the
theory by friends or opponents.
[18] It is clear from the whole context that by "love" I refer to Freud's
early formulation, in which love was used in the popular sense as being
identical with sexuality, including the pregenital; it would have been
clearer if I had written "self-preservation and sexuality." (1970)
[19] "Just as the wild beast must contend with nature to satisfy his needs,
maintain his life and reproduce, so the civilized man must do the same
thing in all the forms of society and with every possible means of production. As he develops, the range of his natural needs broadens, *because* his
needs do; but the productive capabilities, which satisfy these needs, also
expand" (Marx, *Das Kapital*, Hamburg, 1922, III, 2, p. 355, italics mine).

of various drives and needs.[20] However, they never maintained that the "acquisitive drive," the passion for acquisition as an aim in itself, was the only or essential need. To proclaim it a universal human drive would be naively to absolutize a psychic trait that has taken on uncommon force in capitalist society.

Marx and Engels are the last people to whom one would impute the idea of transfiguring bourgeois and capitalist traits into a universal human trait. They were well aware of the place psychology had within sociology, but they neither were nor wanted to be psychologists. Moreover, apart from indications in the French enlightenment literature (especially Helvetius), which should not, of course, be underestimated, they had no scientific materialist psychology at their disposal. Psychoanalysis was the first to provide this psychology, and showed that the "acquisitive drive," although important, did not play a predominant role in man's psychic armament by comparison with other (genital, sadistic, narcissistic) needs. Psychoanalysis, in fact, indicates that in large measure the "acquisitive drive" is not the deepest cause of the need to acquire or possess things; it is rather the expression of a narcissistic need or wish to win recognition from oneself and others. In a society that pays the highest recognition and admiration to the rich man, the narcissistic needs of the society's members inevitably lead to extraordinary intensification of the desire for possessions. On the other hand, in a society where services performed for the whole society rather than property are the basis of social esteem, the same narcissistic impulses will find expression as a "drive" to contribute to society in some important way. Since narcissistic needs are among the most elemental and powerful psychic strivings, it is most important to recognize that the goals (hence the concrete content) of these narcissistic aspirations depend on the specific structure of a society. The imposing role of the "acquisitive drive," then, is largely due to the especially high valuation of property in bourgeois society.

When the materialistic view of history talks about economic causes—apart from the meaning we have just

[20] In *Marx's Contribution to the Knowledge of Man* I have corrected this view and have shown that Marx had a much more elaborate psychology than indicated in the text. (1970)

explained—it is not talking about economics as a subjective psychological motive but as an objective influence on man's activity in life.[21] All man's activity, the satisfying of all his needs, depends on the specific nature of natural economic conditions around; and it is these conditions that determine how man shall live his life. For Marx, man's consciousness is to be explained in terms of his existence in society, in terms of his real, earthly life that is conditioned by the state of his productive capabilities.

> The production of ideas, conceptions and consciousness is directly interwoven with the material activity of men; and material activity is an expression of their real life. Their thoughts and intellectual ideas are seen to be the direct outflow of their material activity. The same holds true for the intellectual productions that find expression in politics, law, morality, religion, metaphysics, etc. Men are the producers of their conceptions and ideas, but we are talking about real, concrete men who are conditioned by the specific way in which their productive capabilities and their corresponding intercourse develops. Consciousness can never be anything but conscious being, and man's being is his concrete life.[22]

Historical materialism sees history as the process of man's active and passive adaptation to the natural conditions around him. "Work is, first and foremost, a process between man and nature, a process in which man mediates, regulates and controls his interaction with nature through his own actions. Vis-à-vis the natural elements themselves, he is a natural force."[23]

Man and nature are the two poles here, interacting with each other, conditioning each other, and altering each other. The historical process is always bound up with man's own nature, and natural conditions outside man. Although Marx stressed the fact that man greatly altered

[21] In his *Economic and Philosophical Manuscripts*, not yet published at the time when this paper was written, Marx makes the point very explicit. He writes ". . . the only wheels that political economy *sets in motion*, are greed . . ." Even a scholar with the best intentions of being objective, R. Tucker, was influenced by the widely-held opinion that Marx assumed greed to be a *primary* motive so that he mistranslated the (difficult) German passage to mean the opposite, namely "the only wheels that *set* political economy in motion are greed." (R. Tucker, *Philosophy and Myth in Karl Marx*, Cambridge Univ. Press, 1961.) (1970)

[22] Marx and Engels, Part I of *Deutschen Ideologie;* Marx-Engels Archives, Band I, p. 239.

[23] Marx, *Das Kapital, op. cit.*, p. 140.

both himself and nature in the historical process, he always emphasized that all such changes were tied up with the existing natural conditions. This is precisely what distinguishes his standpoint from certain idealist positions that accord unlimited power to the human will.[24] As Marx and Engels said,

> The presuppositions with which we begin are not arbitrary dogmas. They are real presuppositions, from which one can abstract only in imagination. They involve real, living individuals, their actions, and the material living conditions which they find or have created. Thus these presuppositions are verifiable in a purely empirical way.

> The first presupposition of human history is, of course, the existence of living human individuals. So the first fact to be verified is the physical organization of these individuals and the resultant relationship between them and nature. Here we cannot go into the physical nature of man nor the varied (geological, climatic, etc.) natural conditions he finds around him. Every description of history must start with these natural foundations, and their modification in the course of history by man's activity.[25]

After the correction of the most drastic misunderstandings, what emerges as the relation between psychoanalysis and historical materialism?

Psychoanalysis can enrich the overall conception of historical materialism on one specific point. *It can provide a more comprehensive knowledge of one of the factors that is operative in the social process: the nature of man himself.* It locates man's instinctual apparatus among the natural factors that modify the social process, although there are also limits to this modifiability. Man's instinctual apparatus is one of the "natural" conditions that forms part of the substructure (*Unterbau*) of the social process. But we are not talking about the instinctual apparatus "in general," or in some pristine biological form, since it is

[24] On this point, see the work of Bucharin that underlines the natural factor in a clear way: *Die Theorie des historischen Materialismus*, 1922. This whole question is specifically dealt with in the illuminating work of K. A. Wittfogel, "Goepolitik, geographischer Materialismus und Marxismus," *Unter dem Banner des Marxismus* III, 1, 4, 5.

[25] Marx and Engels, *op. cit.*, p. 237 f.

only manifest in some *specific* form that has been modified through the social process. The human psyche—or the libidinal forces at its root—are part of the substructure; but they are not the whole substructure, as a psychologistic interpretation would have it. The human psyche always remains a psyche that has been modified by the social process. Historical materialism calls for a psychology—i.e., a science of man's psychic structure; and psychoanalysis is the first discipline to provide a psychology that historical materialism can really use.

The contribution of psychoanalysis is particularly important for the following reasons. Marx and Engels postulated the dependence of all ideological processes on the economic substructure. They saw intellectual and psychic creations as "the material basis reflected in man's head." In many instances, to be sure, historical materialism could provide the right answers without any psychological presuppositions. But only where ideology was the *immediate* expression of economic interests; or where one was trying to establish the correlation between economic substructure and ideological superstructure. Lacking a satisfactory psychology, Marx and Engels could not explain *how* the material basis was reflected in man's head and heart.

Psychoanalysis can show that man's ideologies are the products of certain wishes, instinctual drives, interests, and needs, which themselves, in large measure, unconsciously find expression as rationalizations—i.e., as ideologies. Psychoanalysis can show that while the instinctual drives do develop on the basis of biologically determined instincts, their quantity and content are greatly affected by the individual's socio-economic situation or class. Marx says that men are the producers of their ideologies; analytical social psychology can describe empirically the process of the production of ideologies, of the interaction of "natural" and social factors. *Hence psychoanalysis can show how the economic situation is transformed into ideology via man's drives.*

An important point to note is the fact that this interaction between instincts and environment results in changes within man himself, just as his work changes extra-human nature. Here we can only suggest the general direction of this change. It involves, as Freud has stressed repeatedly, the growth of man's ego organization and the corresponding growth of his capacity for sublimation.[26] Thus psychoanalysis permits us to regard the formation of ideologies as a type of "production process," as another form of the "metabolism" between man and nature. The distinctive aspect here is that "nature" is also within man, not just outside him.

Psychoanalysis can also tell us something about the way ideologies or ideas mold society. It can show that the impact of an idea depends essentially on its unconscious content, which appeals to certain drives; that it is, as it were, the quality and intensity of the libidinal structure of a society which determines the social effect of an ideology.

If it seems clear that psychoanalytic social psychology has a valid place within historical materialism, we can now point to the way in which it can immediately resolve certain difficulties that confront the doctrine of historical materialism.

To begin with, historical materialism can now give a better answer to certain objections. Some opponents, for example, pointed to the role that ideals—e.g., love for the group, the desire for freedom—play in history. Historical materialism could, of course, spurn this type of question as a psychological problem and restrict itself to an analysis of the objective economic conditions that affect historical events. But it was not in a position to explain clearly the nature and source of these real and potent human forces, nor could it explain the role they played in the social process. Psychoanalysis can show that these seemingly ideal motives are actually the rationalized expression of instinctual, libidinous needs and that the content and scope of the dominant needs at any given moment are to be explained in terms of the influence of the socio-economic situation on the instinctual structure of the group that produces the ideology. Hence it is possible for psychoanalysis to reduce the loftiest idealistic motives to their

[26] To me, however, there seems to be an immanent contradiction in Freud's assumption that the growth of the superego and of repressions is tied up with this also, for the growth of the ego and one's capacity for sublimation means that the person gains control over the instincts in other ways rather than through repression.

earthly libidinal nucleus, without having to consider economic needs as the only important ones.[27]

To sum up: (1) The realm of human drives is a natural force which, like other natural forces (soil fertility, natural irrigation, etc.), is an immediate part of the substructure of the social process. Knowledge of this force, then, is necessary for a complete understanding of the social process. (2) The way ideologies are produced and function can only be understood correctly if we know how the system of drives operates. (3) When economically conditioned factors hit upon the realm of drives, some modifications occur; by virtue of the influence of drives, the social process operates at a faster or slower tempo than one would expect if no theoretical consideration to the psychic factors is given.

Thus the use of psychoanalysis within historical materialism will provide a refinement of method, a broader knowledge of the forces at work in the social process, and greater certainty in understanding the course of history and in predicting future historical events. In particular, it will provide a complete understanding of how ideologies are produced.

The fruitfulness of a psychoanalytic social psychology will depend, of course, on the significance of the libidinal forces in the social process. We could not even begin to

---

[27] Lack of any adequate psychology led many proponents of historical materialism to inject a private, purely idealistic psychology in this empty place. A typical example is Kautsky, who, not as openly idealistic as Bernstein and others, assumes that man has an inborn "social instinct," and describes the relationship between this social instinct and social relationships in this way: "Depending on the strength or weakness of his social instinct, man will tend more toward good or evil. But it depends no less on his living conditions in society." (*Op. cit.*, p. 262.) Clearly Kautsky's innate social instinct is nothing less than the innate moral principle; his position differs from idealist ethics only in the way he expresses it.

In his *Theorie des historischen Materialismus*, Bucharin devotes a whole chapter to the problem of psychology. He rightly points out that the psychology of a class is not identical with its "interests"—by which he means its real, economic interests, but that the psychology of a class must always be explained in terms of its socio-economic role. As an example, he cites the case where a mood of despair grips the masses or some group after a great defeat in the class struggle. "Then we can detect a connection with class interests, but this connection is of a distinctive sort: the battle was carried on by the *hidden motives* of the parties involved, and now their army lies in defeat; from this situation arises confusion and despair, and the people begin to look for miracles from heaven" (italics mine).

Bucharin then goes on to say: "In considering class psychology, then, it is evident that we are dealing with a very complicated phenomenon that cannot be explained on the basis of naked interest alone. It must be explained in terms of the concrete milieu of the class in question." Bucharin also notes that ideological processes are a particular type of social labor. But since he has no suitable psychology available to him, he cannot go on to explain the nature of this labor process.

treat this topic thoroughly in this article, so I shall content myself with a few basic suggestions and indications.

Suppose we ask which forces maintain the stability of a given society and which undermine it. We can see that economic prosperity and social conflicts determine stability or decomposition, respectively. But we can also see that the factor which, on the basis of these conditions, serves as a most important element in the social structure are the libidal tendencies actually operative in men. Consider first a relatively stable social constellation. What holds people together? What enables them to have a certain feeling of solidarity, to adjust to the role of ruling or being ruled? To be sure, it is the external power apparatus (police, law courts, army, etc.) that keeps the society from coming apart at the seams. To be sure, it is rational and egotistic interests that contribute to structural stability. But neither the external power apparatus nor rational interests would suffice to guarantee the functioning of the society, if the libidinal strivings of the people were not involved. They serve as the "cement," as it were, without which the society would not hold together, and which contributes to the production of important social ideologies in every cultural sphere.

Let us apply this principle to an especially important social constellation: class relationships. In history as we know it, a minority rules over the majority of society. This class rule was not the result of cunning and deceit, but was a necessary result of the total economic situation of society, of its productive forces. As Necker saw it: "Through the laws of property, the proletariat were condemned to get the barest minimum for their labor." Or, as Linguet put it, they were "to a certain extent, a conspiracy against the majority of the human race, who could find no recourse against them."[28]

The Enlightenment described and criticized this dependency relationship, even though it did not realize that it was economically conditioned. Indeed, minority rule is a historical fact; but what factors allowed this dependency relationship to become stabilized?

First, of course, it was the use of physical force and the

[28] Cited by Grünberg in *Verhandlungen des Vereins für Sozialpolitik*, Stuttgart, 1924, p. 31.

availability of these physical means to certain groups. But there was another important factor at work: the libidinal ties—anxiety, love, trust—which filled the souls of the majority in their relationships with the ruling class. Now this psychic attitude is not the product of whim or accident. It is the expression of people's libidinal adaptation to the conditions of life imposed by economic necessity. So long as these conditions necessitate minority rule over the majority, the libido adapts itself to this economic structure and serves as one of the factors that lend stability to the class relationship.

Besides recognizing the *economic conditions* of the libido structure, social psychology should not forget to investigate the *psychological basis* of this structure. It must explore, not only why this libido structure necessarily exists, but also how it is psychologically possible and through what mechanisms it operates. Exploring the roots of the majority's libidinal ties to the ruling minority, social psychology might discover that this tie is a repetition or continuation of the child's psychic attitude toward his parents, particularly toward his father, in a bourgeois family.[29] We find a mixture of admiration, fear, faith, and confidence in the father's strength and wisdom, briefly, an affectively conditioned reflection of his intellectual and moral qualities, and we find the same in adults of a patriarchal class society vis-à-vis the members of the ruling class. Related to this are certain moral principles which entice the poor to suffer rather than to do wrong, and which lead them to believe that the purpose of their life is to obey their rulers and do their duty. Even these ethical conceptions, which are so important for social stability, are the products of certain affective and emotional relations to those who create and represent such norms.

To be sure, the creation of these norms is not left to chance. One whole basic part of the cultural apparatus serves to form the socially required attitude in a systematic and methodical way. It is an important task of social psychology to analyze the functions of the whole educa-

---

[29] It should be remembered that this specific father-child relationship itself is socially conditioned.

tional system and other systems (such as the penal system) in this process.[80]

We have focused on the libidinal relationships between the ruling minority and the ruled majority because this factor is the social and psychic core of every class society. But other social relationships, too, bear their own distinctive libidinal stamp. The relationships between members of the same class have a different psychic coloring in the lower middle class than they do in the proletariat. Or, the relationship to the political leader who identifies with his class and serves their interests even while he leads them, from what it is when he confronts them as a strong man, as the great father who rules as omnipotent authority.[81]

The diversity of possible libidinal relationships is matched by the wide variety of possible emotional relationships within society. Even a brief sketch is impossible here; this problem would indeed, be a major task for an analytic social psychology. Let me just point out that every society has its own distinctive *libidinal structure*, even as it has its own economic, social, political, and cultural structure. This libidinal structure is the product of the influence of socio-economic conditions on human drives; in turn, it is an important factor conditioning emotional developments within the various levels of society, and the contents of the "ideological superstructure." The libidinal structure of a society is the medium through which the economy exerts its influence on man's intellectual and mental manifestations.[82]

Of course, the libidinal structure of a society does not

[80] See Fromm, "Zur Psychologie des Verbrechers und der strafenden Gesellschaft," XVII, *Imago*, 12. Not only does the cultural apparatus serve to direct the libido forces (especially the pregenital and the partial drives) in specific, socially desired directions. It also serves to weaken the libido forces to the point where they no longer are a threat to social stability. This toning down of the libido forces—i.e., turning them back into the pregenital realm—is one of the motives of the sexual morality of the given society.

[81] In *Mass Psychology and Ego-Analysis*, Freud focuses on the libido factors in the relationship to the leader. But he takes both "leader" and "masses" in an abstract sense, disregarding the concrete situation surrounding them. He thus gives a universality to the psychic processes involved that does not correspond to reality. In other words, he turns one particular type of relationship to the leader into a universal type. Another critical problem of social psychology, class relationships, is replaced by a secondary problem: the ruler-mass relationship. It is noteworthy, however, that in this work Freud notes the general tendency of bourgeois social psychology to disparage the masses, and does not fall in with it.

[82] What I have called here the "libidinal structure" of society, using Freudian terminology, I have in my later work called the "social character"; in spite of the change in the libido theory, the concepts are the same. (1970)

remain constant, no more than does its economic and
social structure. But it remains relatively constant so long
as the social structure retains a certain equilibrium—i.e.,
during the phase of relative consolidation in the society's
development. With the growth of objective contradictions
and conflicts within the society, and with the acceleration
of the disintegration process, certain changes in the society's libidinal structure also take place. We see the disap-
pearance of traditional ties that maintained the stability of
the society; there is change in traditional emotional attitudes. Libidinal energies are freed for new uses, and thus
change their social function. They no longer serve the
preservation of the society, but contribute to the development of new social formations. They cease to be "cement," and turn into dynamite.

Let us return to the question we were discussing at the
beginning: the relationship of the drives to life experiences—i.e., to the objective conditions of life. We have
seen that analytic individual psychology views instinctual
development as the result of the active and passive adaptation of the instinctual apparatus to the actual conditions
of life. In principle, the same relationship holds true between a society's libidinal structure and its economic conditions: it is a process of active and passive adaptation of
the society's libidinal structure to the existing economic
conditions. Human beings, driven by their libidinous impulses, bring about changes in the economic conditions;
the changed economic conditions cause new libidinal goals
and satisfactions to arise. The decisive point is that all
these changes ultimately go back to the economic conditions, that the drives and needs change and adapt themselves in accordance with economic conditions.

Clearly, analytic psychology has its place within the
framework of historical materialism. It investigates one of
the natural factors that is operative in the relationship
between society and nature: the realm of human drives,
and the active and passive role they play within the social
process. Thus it investigates a factor that plays a decisive
mediating role between the economic base and the formation of ideologies. Thus analytic social psychology enables
us to understand fully the ideological superstructure in

terms of the process that goes on between society and man's nature.

Now we can readily summarize the findings of our study on the method and function of a psychoanalytic social psychology. Its method is that of classical Freudian psychoanalysis as applied to social phenomena. It explains the shared, socially relevant, psychic attitudes in terms of the process of active and passive adaptation of the apparatus of drives to the socio-economic living conditions of the society.

Its task is, first of all, to analyze the socially relevant libidinal strivings: i.e., to describe the libidinal structure of a given society, and to explain the origin of this structure and its function in the social process. An important element of this work, then, will be the theory explaining how ideologies arise from the interaction of the psychic apparatus and the socio-economic conditions.

9

PSYCHOANALYTIC CHARACTEROLOGY
AND ITS RELEVANCE FOR
SOCIAL PSYCHOLOGY

THE STARTING POINT of psychoanalysis was a therapeutic one. Psychic disturbances were explained in terms of the damming up of sexual energy and its pathological transformation in some symptomatic manifestation; or they were explained as defenses against libido-charged ideas that were not allowed into the person's consciousness. The sequence, libido → defense through repression → symptom, was the Ariadne thread of early analytic investigations. Related to this was the fact that the objects of analytic study were almost exclusively sick people—most of them having physical symptoms.

As psychoanalysis developed, another question also came under study: What was the origin and significance of certain psychic characteristics found in both sick and healthy people? Like the original investigations, these studies sought to uncover the instinctual, libidinous roots of psychic attitudes. But now the sequence did not run from repression to *symptom;* it ran from sublimation (or reaction formation) to *character trait.* Such investigations necessarily proved fruitful for our understanding of both sick and healthy character types; thus they became especially important for the problem studied in social psychology.

The general basis of psychoanalytic characterology is to view certain character traits as sublimations or reaction

["Psychoanalytic Characterology and Its Relevance for Social Psychology" was first published in the *Zeitschrift für Sozialforschung*, Hirschfeld-Leipzig, 1932.]

formations of certain instinctual drives that are sexual in nature—"sexual" being used in the extended sense that Freud gave to it. This genetic derivation of psychic phenomena from libidinal sources and early childhood experiences is the specifically analytic principle that psychoanalytic characterology shares with the theory of neurosis. But while the neurotic symptom (and the neurotic character) is the result of an unsatisfactory adaptation of the instincts to social reality, one can speak of a non-neurotic character trait when libidinal impulses are transformed into relatively stable and socially adapted traits—through reaction formation or sublimation. In any case, the distinction between normal and neurotic character is quite fluid; it depends primarily on the degree of the lack of social adaptation.

It is important to recall that Freud related the problem of sublimation predominantly to pregenital sexual drives: i.e., oral and anal sexuality, and sadism.[1] The difference between reaction formation and sublimation is essentially that the former always functions to resist and keep down a repressed impulse, from which it draws its energy, while the latter represents a direct transformation, a "canalization" of instinctual impulses.

The theory of pregenital sexuality was treated extensively by Freud for the first time in his *Three Essays on the Theory of Sexuality*. It starts from the observation that even before the genitals play a decisive role for the child, the oral and anal zones—as "erogenous zones"—are the focal point of pleasurable sensations analogous to genital ones. In the course of the child's development, these erogenous zones surrender part of their sexual energy to the genitals, while retaining a smaller share either in its original form or in the form of sublimations and reaction formations within the ego.

Building on these observations about pregenital sexuality, Freud published a brief article, "Character and Anal Eroticism," in 1908,[2] which formed the basis for psychoanalytic characterology. Freud starts from the observation that in analysis one frequently encounters a type of person

---

[1] Thus one greatly misconstrues the Freudian standpoint when he equates the problem of sublimation with the problem of genital-sexual abstinence. This is done, for example, by Scheler in *Wesen und Formen der Sympathie*, Bonn, 1923, pp. 238 ff.

[2] *Ges. Schriften*, V, 260 ff.

who "is distinguished by a combination of specific character traits, while the behavior of a specific bodily function and its associated organs attracts attention to itself in their childhood."[3]

In individuals where pleasure in bowel evacuation and its products play an especially large role in childhood, Freud finds three character traits: orderliness, parsimony and obstinacy. He placed particular stress on the equation of feces and money (gifts) found in neurosis and in many myths, superstitions, dreams, and fairy tales. On the basis of Freud's fundamental study, a number of other psychoanalytic authors have made contributions to psychoanalytic characterology.[4] In many respects, there is one point, however, that is not brought out clearly enough in these works, and will enable us to have a better understanding of these problems. I refer to the distinction between sexual goal and sexual object, or between organ pleasure and object relationships.

Freud establishes a close connection between the sexual drives and the "erogenous zones,"[5] and assumed that the sex drives are called forth by stimulation of these erogenous zones. In the first stage of life, the oral zone and its associated functions—sucking and biting—is the center of sexuality. After the nursing stage, however, this shifts to the anal zone and its functions—stool evacuation or stool retention; then, from three to five, the genital zone gains in importance. Freud designates this first blush of genital sexuality as the "phallic phase," because he assumes that for both sexes it is only the phallus (or the phallically experienced clitoris) that plays a role, along with tendencies toward forceful invasion and destruction. After a period of "latency," which lasts approximately until puberty, genital sexuality develops in association with

[3] Ibid., p. 261.

[4] See the instructive remarks and extensive bibliography of Otto Fenichel, Perversionen, Psychosen, Charakterstorungen: Psychoanalytische spezielle Neurosenlehre, Vienna, 1931.

[5] It is easy to see why Freud attributed a central role to the erogenous zones. Such an assumption readily resulted not only from his empirical observations but also from his theoretical presuppositions, which were those of a mechanistic, physiological standpoint. They exerted a decisive influence on the formulation of psychoanalytic theory. Any fruitful discussion of various psychoanalytic theses would have to begin with a critique of the central role given to the erogenous zones. We shall not undertake such a critique here, since our purpose is to present the findings of psychoanalysis. But it is an important question.

physical maturation. The pregenital sexual strivings are now dominated by, and integrated into, genital sexuality.

It is important to make a distinction between this erogenous lust and the person's object relationships. The latter are the person's (loving or hating) attitudes toward himself or other people he encounters; in a word, they are his emotions, feelings, and attitudes toward the surrounding world in general. These object relationships also have a typical course of development. According to Freud, the suckling infant is predominantly narcissistic and concerned solely with the satisfaction of his own needs and wants. Around the end of the nursing period, a second stage sets in where there is an increase in sadistic, hostile attitudes toward objects; these same attitudes also play an important role in the phallic phase. Only with the growing primacy of genital sexuality in puberty do loving, friendly attitudes toward objects clearly become dominant.

These object relationships are seen as having a very close connection with the erogenous zones. The connection is understandable when we consider the fact that specific object relationships first develop in connection with specific erogenous zones and that these connections are not fortuitous. At this point I really do not want to raise the whole question as to whether the connection is really as close as much of the psychoanalytic literature would have it; nor do I want to consider whether and to what extent an object relationship, typical of a particular erogenous zone, can also develop independently of the particular fate of that zone. So let me just lay stress on the importance of making a basic distinction between organ pleasure and object relationships.[6]

In the first stage of life, the central sexual drive is *oral eroticism*. In the infant there is a strong feeling of pleasure and satisfaction, originally associated with sucking; later it is associated with biting, chewing, taking things into the mouth, and wanting to swallow them up. Closer observation shows that this is definitely not an expression of hunger; that the very activities of sucking, biting, and swallowing up are pleasurable activities in themselves.

[6] This paper, like the two others of 1932 and 1934 published in this volume, is written from the standpoint of acceptance of Freud's libido theory, and thus does not conform any longer with my present point of view. Nevertheless, in the foregoing paragraphs, as well as in some other points, critical questions are raised which are the basis for my later revisions of classic theory. (1970)

Although the direct oral-erotic needs and satisfactions wane after the nursing period, more or less large vestiges of them are retained in later childhood and adulthood. We need only think of the prolongation of such habits as thumb-sucking and nail-biting, to the perfectly "normal" practice of kissing, and to the libidinous, oral-erotic roots of smoking.

Insofar as oral eroticism is not retained in its original form or superseded by other sexual impulses, it appears in reaction formations or sublimations. Here we shall just mention the most significant example of such sublimation: the transfer of the infant's sucking pleasure to the intellectual realm. Knowledge takes the place of mother's milk; we commonly use such expressions as "drinking at the breasts of wisdom." This symbolic equation of drinking and intellectual receptiveness is found in the language and fairy tales of various cultures as well as in the dreams and associations of psychoanalytic patients. As far as *reaction formations* are concerned, they can remain unsublimated, as in inhibitions about eating, or be sublimated in inhibitions about learning, working, being curious, etc.

The object relationships that appear in the first stage of infant life are extremely complicated.[7] At first the infant is narcissistically oriented—extremely so in the first three months of life; there is no distinction between the self and the world outside. Gradually, loving and friendly attitudes toward objects develop alongside this narcissistic attitude.[8] The attitude of the infant toward the mother (or mother substitute) becomes friendly and loving; the infant expects love and protection. Mother is its guarantee of life, and her love provides a feeling of protection and security. To be sure, she is in large measure the means by which the child's needs are satisfied; and the child's love is in large measure composed of wanting and taking rather than giving and caring. Nevertheless, the child's traits of loving and being interested in other objects are important in this first stage.[9]

---

[7] See Bernfeld, *Psychologie des Säuglings*, Vienna, 1925.

[8] In the psychoanalytic literature, stress is laid on the narcissistic attitude of the young child, while his friendly attitude toward others is given short shrift. I shall not delve into this important problem here, except to point to the existence of such friendly traits together with the hateful, sadistic ones.

[9] It should be obvious that in the whole process of human development we can only talk about an increase or decrease of various tendencies, not about the clear-cut alternation of sharply separate structural types.

The child's object relationships gradually change. As his bodily growth proceeds, so do his demands. Because of this fact and because of other factors in the environment, he increasingly encounters frustrations in the world around him. To these frustrations, the child reacts with anger and rage, and his physical growth has created conditions that facilitate these manifestations. Alongside and in place of his friendly orientation toward other objects, hostile feelings enter in increasing measure. Feeling stronger in himself and raging over various disappointments, the child no longer trusts in loving satisfaction of his wishes, which are still primarily oral in character. He no longer waits for such satisfaction to come to him; he begins to try to take by force what is denied him. The mouth and teeth become his weapon. He develops an aggressive attitude, which looks on objects with hostility; he wants to attack them, devour them, destroy them. Conflicts and aggressive-sadistic impulses take the place of the relative harmony that originally marked his relationship with the surrounding environment.[10]

These, then, are the elements that come together to form the "oral" character traits of adults: on the one hand, an attitude of trust and friendship toward others, a desire to be loved and pampered; and on the other hand, continuation into aggressive, hate-filled, predatory tendencies.

Abraham makes a distinction between the characterological consequences of two different childhood situations. The first is one where the child's oral satisfactions are undisturbed and happy. The second situation is one where much disturbance and displeasure are intermingled: e.g., sudden separation from the breast, insufficient milk, or, in terms of object relationships, a lack of love on the part of the mothering person. People who come from the first childhood situation and its happy connotations

have often brought along a deep-rooted conviction that things must always go well for them. They face life with an unshakeable optimism, which often helps them to actually attain their practical goals. Even here, however, there can be a less fortunate type of development. Many people fully

[10] Here we cannot delve into such questions as to what extent the will to devour things and possess things are primitive tendencies of man in relationship to the environment.

expect that there will always be a good, caring person around, i.e., a mother substitute, from whom they will certainly get all the necessities of life. This optimistic faith in their destiny condemns them to inactivity. Among these people we see those who were pampered in childhood. Their whole behavior in life shows that they expect to drink at mother's breast forever. Such persons make no personal efforts. In many cases, they disdain any notion of personal achievement.[11]

In these people we frequently note a marked liberality, a certain lordly manner. Their ideal is the mother who gives unreservedly, and they try to live up to this ideal.

People who come from the second childhood situation mentioned above suffered deep oral frustrations. In later life they frequently develop traits that have to do with robbing other people or sucking them dry. They seem to walk around with a long trunk, sucking up everything in sight. When correspondingly strong sadistic tendencies are intermingled, they go around like beasts of prey looking for victims to devour.

In their social behavior, they are always demanding something for themselves, either pleading or commanding. The way they make their requests has an aura of tenacious sucking about it. Neither facts nor rational objections can put them off. They keep pushing and insisting. It is as if they really meant to attach themselves to other people like leeches. They are particularly sensitive about being alone, and react against it, even when only a short time is involved. Impatience is particularly evident in these people. Among some people of this type, the behavior just mentioned takes on a more cruel aspect. Their attitude towards other human beings has something of the vampire about it.[12]

The first type of person described above evinces a certain nobility and magnanimity; he is serenely merry and sociable. The second type is hostile and sarcastic, reacting with rage when his requests are denied and deeply envious of those who have it better than he does. Another fact noted by Abraham is of particular importance to sociologists: persons with an oral character

[11] Karl Abraham, *Psychoanalytische Studien zur Charakterbildung*, Vienna, 1925, p. 42.
[12] *Ibid.*, p. 44.

formation are readily open to new things, "while those with an anal character formation have a conservative attitude that is hostile to any and all innovation . . ."

Anal eroticism does not begin to play a role until only *after* the period of oral eroticism. Right from the start, the unrestricted discharge of body products is associated with pleasurable stimulation of the anal mucous membrane in the child. In like manner, the evacuated products—their appearance, their smell, their contact with the surface of the trunk, and hand contact with them—are a source of intensely pleasurable sensations. The infant is proud of his feces; it is his first "possession," the embodiment of his first productivity.

A basic change takes place with the ongoing toilet-training of the child, which presupposes the gradually developing function of the bladder and anal sphincters. As the child adapts himself to the new demands of the training, as he learns to hold back his stools and let them go at the right time, the retention of his stools and the associated physiological processes become a new source of pleasure. His original love for feces is, to some extent, replaced by feelings of disgust; but the primitive pride in the feces is partly increased by the pride of those around him in his punctual evacuation.

As is the case with the original oral impulses, a portion of the anal impulses is retained to some extent in the life of the adult. This fact is readily recognizable in the relatively strong affective reactions of many people to the anal insult and the anal joke. The vestiges of earlier anal eroticism can also be seen clearly in people's loving interest in their own feces, which appears under all sorts of rationalizations. But normally a substantial portion of anal-erotic strivings merge into sublimations and reaction formations.

The further development of the child's original anal eroticism lies in a twofold direction: (1) in the characterological continuation of the original functions, which results in pleasure or inability to retain, collect and produce; furthermore in the development of orderliness, punctuality, cleanliness, and stinginess; (2) in the continuation of the original love for feces, which finds expression primarily in love for possessions. Particular significance is attached to the feeling of duty that develops during this stage. Anal weaning is closely tied up with the problem of "must," "should," and "ought not"; and clinical experience shows that exceptionally intense feelings about a sense of duty often go back to this early stage.

The object relationships associated with the anal stage are marked by growing conflict with the surrounding world. Now, for the first time, the environment confronts the child with demands, whose fulfillment is enforced with rewards or punishments. When mother approaches the child, she is no longer the good, self-giving one who provides and ensures pleasure; now she is someone who frustrates and punishes. The child reacts accordingly. He remains fixed in his narcissistic, indifferent attitude, which is heightened to some extent by his diminishing physical helplessness and his growing pride in his own accomplishments. At the same time there is a marked increase in his stubborn, sadistic, hostile attitude toward others, and his angry defense against all invasions into his private life.

The sublimations and reaction formations of anal eroticism, and the continuation of the object relations that are typically associated with this stage, combine to form the anal character traits described in psychoanalytic literature in both their normal and pathological manifestations. Here I shall simply allude to several traits particularly important for social psychology.

I have already mentioned the first characterological findings of Freud: a love of orderliness that often runs over into pedantry, a parsimony that borders on stinginess and avarice, and a stubbornness bordering on insolent defiance. A host of psychoanalytic writers, Jones and Abraham in particular, have added many more details to these general traits. Abraham points to certain overcompensations for this original stubbornness,

> under which the original stubborn maintenance of the right to self-determination lies hidden, until it bursts out into the open now and then. I am thinking here of certain children and adults who display special goodness, correctness and obedience, but explain their deep underlying rebelliousness by the fact that it was suppressed in their early life.[13]

Closely associated with pride is their feeling of unique-

[13] Ibid., p. 9.

ness that was first underlined by Sadger: "Anything that is not Me is dirt." Such people enjoy a possession only if no one else has anything like it. They are inclined to regard everything in life as property and to protect everything that is "private" from outside invasions. This attitude does not apply to money and possessions only; it also applies to human beings, feelings, memories, and experiences. The strength of the underlying libidinous tendencies, which associate property with the private sphere, can readily be gauged by their rage over any invasion into their private life, their "freedom." Here, too, belongs a trait noted by Abraham: the sensitivity of the anal character to any outside invasion. No one is to butt into "their business."

Related to this is also another trait noted by Jones: the stubborn maintenance of a self-devised regimen, or the tendency to force such a regimen on others.[14] Such people frequently exhibit unusual delight in devising ritual schedules, tables, and plans. Of particular importance is the fact (stressed by Abraham) that the anal character exhibits an unconscious tendency to regard the anal function as the most important productive activity and as something superior to the genital function. Earning money, accumulating possessions, amassing bits and pieces of knowledge without transforming them into something productive—all these are expressions of this attitude.[15]

Along with their high estimation of anal, accumulating productivity there is characteristically a high esteem for possessions and things accumulated. As Abraham notes:

In marked cases of anal character formation, almost all the relationships of life are viewed in terms of having (keeping)

[14] One mother draws up a written program in which she minutely details her daughter's day. The morning, for example, is divided up as follows: (1) out of bed, (2) potty, (3) washing, etc. From time to time during the morning, she knocks on her daughter's door and asks: How far are you? The little girl is supposed to respond: I'm at 9 (or 15, or whatever). Thus the mother keeps tight control over the execution of the daily program (*ibid.*, p. 12).

[15] "Such people like to give money and similar gifts. Many of them play the benefactor or the philanthropist. But their libido remains more or less distant from the objects, so their work efforts are essentially unproductive. They certainly do not lack perseverance—a common trait of the anal character—but they utilize it in unproductive ways to a large extent. For example, they may stubbornly hold on to established forms in an unproductive way. If the worst comes to worst, their interest in content gives way to an interest in purely formal procedure" *Ibid.*, p. 18.

and giving: i.e., in terms of possessions. It is as if the motto of many such people were: "The person who gives something to me is my friend; the person who demands something from me is my enemy."[16]

The case is no different with their love relationships. With people of an anal character it is characteristic that genital need and genital satisfaction are restricted to a greater or lesser extent. This restrictedness is frequently accompanied by moralistic rationalizations or anxieties. To the extent that love does play a role, it takes a typical form. A woman is not loved, she is "possessed." The emotional feeling toward the "love" object is the same as that toward other objects of possession: i.e., there is a tendency to possess as much and as exclusively as possible.

The first attitude (possessing as much as possible) is to be seen in a type of person who seems quite capable of love, but whose love is basically just another form of the passion to collect. A particularly telling example of the first attitude was offered by one client of mine, who had a scrapbook in which he placed all the souvenirs of his encounters with women—and there were many: theater programs, used tickets, letters, etc. The second attitude (possessing as exclusively as possible) we find in a type of person who is extremely jealous and concerned with "fidelity."

Closely associated with this attitude is the intense envy that is found in many people with an anal character. They use up their strength, not in productive activity of their own, but in envying the achievements and (above all) the possessions of others. This brings us again to one of the anal characteristics that is most important clinically and sociologically: their particular relationship toward money and, above all, their parsimony and stinginess. This particular trait has been widely confirmed by psychoanalytic experiences, and it has been treated extensively in the pertinent literature.[16a]

[16] Ibid., p. 20.
[16a] Here a few remarks of Abraham are noteworthy: There are cases where the connection between deliberate stool-retention and systematic thriftiness is perfectly obvious. I know of a rich banker who always urges his children to retain their bowel movements as long as possible, so as to derive as much benefit as possible from the food they have eaten.
Also noteworthy is the fact that many neurotics restrict their parsimony to specific types of expenditure, but are quite free with their money

Parsimony and avarice do not relate solely to money and monetary values. Time and energy are treated in a similar way, and such people abhor any waste of either.[17] It is worth noting that these anal tendencies are subjected to extensive rationalizations. Economic considerations, of course, are the first to be put forth. Also noteworthy is the fact that alongside the keen concern for cleanliness, parsimony, orderliness, and punctuality, we frequently see breaking through the very opposite traits, which had been kept down through these reaction formations. Lastly, because of its relevance for social psychology, we should mention Abraham's reference to the characteristic need of the anal character for symmetry and "proper balance."

In principle, *genital sexuality* has a different significance for character formation than do oral and anal sexuality. While only a relatively small measure of the latter can survive the period of early childhood in direct form, and are chiefly applied to sublimations and reaction formations in later life, genital sexuality is primarily designed to maintain direct physical discharge. Simple as it is to describe the sexual goal of genital sexuality, it is difficult to say anything about the specifically genital character traits. It is certainly true that the object relationship attached to

---

in other areas. There are patients, for example, who refuse to spend money on "transitory" things. A concert or a journey costs money, and one gets no permanent possession from the expense. I know one person who avoided going to the opera for this reason, but readily spent money for the sheet music of arias he had not heard; the latter was something permanent that he could hold on to. Many such neurotics are reluctant to spend money for food, because it does not remain as a permanent possession. Another type is quite willing to spend money for nourishment, in which they show extraordinary interest. Such people are deeply interested in the care of their body, their weight, etc. They are really concerned to know how much of what they imbibe remains as a lasting possession. It is evident that these people equate body content with money.

In other cases we find an attitude of parsimony towards their whole way of living. Sometimes this is carried to such extremes that they fret over negligible economies. I know one man who used to run around the house with his trousers open, in order to save the buttonholes. One can readily guess that other drives are at work here also, but it is characteristic that they can hide themselves underneath the anal tendency of thrift.

In many patients we find a specialized form of this thriftiness: they are very economical in their use of toilet paper. Here the co-determining factor is the dread of soiling clean things [*ibid.*, p. 22-23].

[17] "Many neurotics are terribly worried about wasting time. Only time spent on work seems to be time well spent. Any interruption of their work irritates them greatly. They hate inactivity and pleasure. These are the same people whom Ferenczi describes as 'Sunday neurotics.' They can brook no interruption in their work. As in the case of many such neurotically motivated tendencies, they often fall short of their goal. They save time in small things, and waste it in important things" (p. 23).

genital sexuality is one of friendliness and relative freedom from ambivalence.[18] But it should not be forgotten that a physiologically normal sex act does not necessarily imply the corresponding psychic attitude of love. From the psychological standpoint, it can be experienced as predominantly narcissistic or sadistic.

If we turn to the characterologically important reaction formations and sublimations of genital sexuality, the formation of will seems to be the first important reaction formation. As far as sublimations are concerned, I think it necessary to distinguish between male and female sexuality. (One should not forget, however, that both masculine and feminine sexual impulses exist in every individual.)[19]

We still know very little about their sublimations. We may perhaps conjecture that the sublimation of masculine sexuality tends predominantly toward intellectual effort, creation, and synthesis and that the sublimation of feminine sexuality tends toward assimilating, sheltering, producing, and showing unconditional motherly love.[20]

We have briefly sketched the psychoanalytic theory concerning the development of sexuality and object relationships. It is still a rough schema that is hypothetical in many respects. Further analytic research will have to alter many important points and introduce many new ones. But it is a starting point that enables us to understand the instinctual basis of character traits, and opens the way for us to explain the *development* of character.

This development is conditioned by two factors that operate in different directions. The first is the physical maturation of the individual. This means, first and foremost, the growth of genital sexuality and the physiologically diminishing role of the oral and anal zones; it also means the maturation of the whole personality and the concomitant diminution of helplessness, enabling the person to develop an attitude of friendliness and love toward others.

The second factor that contributes to the process of development operates on the individual from without. It is

[18] This raises a central problem, the psychology of love, which has not been really tackled yet by psychoanalysis.

[19] See Freud's observations in his *Three Essays on the Theory of Sexuality*, Leipzig, 1923, p. 16, n.

[20] The problems touched upon here lead to questions that are little discussed within psychoanalysis. See Wilhelm Reich, "Der genitale und der neurotische Charakter," *Int. Zeitschrift für Psychoanalyse* (1929).

composed of the social rules, transmitted most vividly through the educational process, which call for the repression of pregenital sexual strivings in large measure and thus facilitate the forward march of genital sexuality.

Frequently, however, this march is never fully completed. Either in a direct or sublimated form, the pregenital areas remain extraordinarily strong. There are two basic reasons why pregenital aspirations may remain so strong: (1) fixation—because of the especially strong satisfaction or rejection experienced in childhood, pregenital wishes resist the maturation process and maintain their power; (2) regression—after the normal process of development has ended, a particularly severe internal or external frustration leads the person to turn back from love and genitality to the earlier pregenital stages of libido organization. In reality, fixation and regression ordinarily work together. A given fixation represents a disposition which, under certain circumstances, can readily bring about a regression to the fixated instinctual stage.

By pointing out the libidinal basis of character traits, psychoanalytic characterology can help to explain their dynamic function as productive forces in society. On the other hand, it can also serve as the starting point for a social psychology that will show how the character traits common to most members of a society are conditioned by the distinctive nature of that society.

This social influence on character formation operates first and foremost through the family; it is the chief medium through which the child's psychic formation is oriented toward the surrounding society. In what way and to what degree a child's pregenital strivings are suppressed or intensified, and the manner in which sublimations or reaction formations are stimulated, depends basically on the educational process—the latter being an expression of the overall society's psychic structure.

But society's influence on the formation of character extends beyond childhood. Certain character traits are the most useful—and do most to advance the individual— within a given economic, social or class structure. For these traits there is something that we can call a "social reward"; it operates to insure the adaptation of the individual's character to what is considered "normal" and "healthy" within the given social structure.[21] Character development, then, involves the adaptation of the libido structure to a given social structure—first through the medium of the family, and then through direct contact with social life.

Here the sexual morality of a society plays a very special role. As we pointed out, the major portions of the individual's pregenital strivings fade away into genital sexuality. To the extent that the sexual morality of a given society restricts genital satisfaction, there must be a corresponding intensification of pregenital impulses or their concomitant character traits. When stress is placed on prohibitions against genital satisfaction, the libido flows backward to the pregenital zones and we see increased evidence of oral and anal character traits in the life of the society.

Since character traits are anchored in the libidinal structure, they remain relatively stable. They develop as adaptations to the given economic and social structure, to be sure, but they do not disappear as fast as these structures and relationships change. The libidinal structure, from which these character traits develop, has a certain inertia; a long period of adaptation to new economic conditions is required before we get a corresponding change in the libidinal structure and its consequent character traits. This is the reason why the ideological superstructure, which is based on the character traits typical of a given society, changes more slowly than the economic substructure.

At this point I shall try to apply the findings of psychoanalytic characterology to a concrete sociological problem. My remarks are simply meant as an illustration of the way to proceed in these matters, not as a definitive answer to the problem broached.

The problem of the "spirit"—i.e., the psychic basis—of capitalism seems to be a particularly suitable example for two reasons. First, because the most relevant part of psychoanalytic characterology for an understanding of the bourgeois spirit—the theory about the anal character—

[21] The distinction between "normal" and "neurotic" character traits is itself conditioned by social factors to a large extent. It can only be dealt with in connection with a specific society: any character structure that is not adapted to this society is "sick." The character of a nineteenth-century capitalist merchant would seem quite "sick" to a feudal society, and vice versa.

happens to be the most developed part of psychoanalytic characterology. Second, because there is an extended sociological literature concerning this problem, so that the introduction of a new viewpoint seems in order.

What do I mean by the "spirit" of capitalism (or of bourgeois society)? I mean the sum total of character traits that are typical of human beings in this society—the emphasis being on the dynamic function of character. I use "character" here in a very broad sense and by and large I could use Sombart's definition of the "spirit" of an economic system. He defines it as "the sum total of psychic characteristics that are involved in economic activities. This would include all the expressions of intellectual life and all the character traits that are present in economic endeavors, as well as all goals, value judgments and principles that affect and regulate the behavior of people engaged in this activity."[22]

Insofar as I am concerned with the spirit of a society or a class, however, my definition goes beyond the spirit relevant for economic activity but refers to the psychic traits of individuals in a given class or society, which, after all, are the same, whether it is a question of economic activity or not. Moreover, in contrast to Sombart, I am not primarily concerned with "principles" and "value judgments" but with the character traits in which they are rooted.

We shall not deal with the problem of the connection between the bourgeois spirit and Protestantism and Protestant sects. This problem is so complex that even a few fleeting observations would lead us too far afield. For the same reason, we shall not explore the *economic* roots of capitalist society. This is methodologically permissible when we are at this point only trying to describe the specific *character* of a society and to study the question how this character—the manifestation of a specific *libidinal structure*—is a productive force which participates in shaping the development of that society. A complete social-psychological investigation would have to start with the description of the economic facts and show how the libidinal structure adapts itself to these facts.

Finally, we shall neglect another complicated and much debated question of a historical nature: At what point in

[22] Sombart, *Der Bourgeois*, Munich and Leipzig, 1913, p. 2.

history can we really begin to talk about capitalism and a bourgeois-capitalist spirit? We shall rather start from the assumption that there is such a spirit and that it has certain uniform traits—whether we meet it first in fifteenth-century Florence (as Sombart claims), or seventeenth-century England, in Defoe, or in Benjamin Franklin, or Andrew Carnegie, and the typical nineteenth-century merchant.[23]

The specific nature of the bourgeois-capitalist spirit can be most readily described in negative terms, by noting the features of the precapitalist spirit (for example, that of the Middle Ages) which it no longer possesses. Getting pleasure and enjoyment out of life is no longer a goal that is taken for granted by the bourgeois psyche, no longer a self-evident purpose that various activities, particularly economic activities, seek to serve. And this holds true whether we are talking about the worldly pleasures enjoyed by the medieval feudal class, the "blessedness" that the Church promised to the masses, or the enjoyment that a person got out of sumptuous festivals, beautiful paintings, and splendid buildings, and a great number of feast days. It was understood that man had an innate right to happiness, blessedness, or pleasure; this was viewed as the proper goal of all human activity, whether it was economic or not.

The bourgeois spirit introduced a decisive change in this respect. Happiness or blessedness ceased to be the unquestioned goal of life. Something else took first place on the scale of values: duty. Kraus regards this as one of the most significant differences between the scholastic and the Calvinist attitude: "The thing that sharply distinguishes Calvin's work ethos from that of the scholastic period is the former's removal of goal-directedness and its emphasis on formal obedience to one's calling in life. The material on which a person was working no longer made any difference. Iron discipline was demanded to act out of a deep feeling of obedience and duty."[24] Despite his many

[23] See in particular: Sombart, Der Bourgeois, Munich 1913; Max Weber, Ges. Aufsätze zur Religionssoziologie, Tübingen, 1920, Vol. I; Tawney, Religion and the Rise of Capitalism, London, 1927; Brentano, Die Anfänge des modernen Kapitalismus, Munich, 1916; Troeltsch, Die Soziallehren der christlichen Kirche, Ges. Schr., Tübingen, 1919, Vol. I; Kraus, Scholastik, Puritanismus und Kapitalismus, Munich and Leipzig, 1930. All have extensive bibliographies for the reader.
[24] Kraus, op. cit., p. 245.

differences with Max Weber, Kraus seconded him on this point: "Weber was certainly right when he noted that 'the primitive church and the Middle Ages had never known the notion that the fulfillment of duty within one's worldly calling is the highest form of ethical self-regulation."[25] The evaluation of duty (in place of happiness or blessedness) as the highest value runs from Calvinism through the whole gamut of bourgeois thought—in either theological or other rationalizations.

Another change occurred when the notion of duty became central. People no longer engaged in economic activity to maintain an appropriate, traditional livelihood; acquiring possessions and saving as such became ethical norms regardless of whether one enjoyed what one had acquired or not. There is so much reference to this fact in the pertinent literature that we need only offer a few suggestive examples.

Sombart mentions the "family books" of the Alberti family as a particularly striking example of the new value placed on savings and economizing. Here are a few quotes:

Avoid superfluous expenditures as you would the plague.

Any expenditure that is not absoutely necessary is madness.

Thriftiness is as praiseworthy and good, as wasteful expenditure is abominable.

Thriftiness hurts no one, and it helps the family.

Thriftiness is a blessing.

Do you know the type of people I like best? Those who spend money only for what is absolutely necessary, and save the surplus; those I call thrifty householders.[26]

Alberti also preaches economy in the use of one's energy:

True *Maserizia* should involve the use of three things that are ours: 1) our soul, 2) our body and, above all, 3) our time!

To avoid wasting this precious commodity, time, I follow the following rule: Never will I give in to laziness. I will shun sleep until I am ready to drop from exhaustion . . .

[25] *Ibid.*
[26] L. B. Alberti, *I libri della famiglia*, Florence, G. Mangini, 1908; cited by Sombart, *op. cit.*, p. 140.

Thus I avoid laziness and sleep by setting some task for myself. To accomplish what must be accomplished, I draw up a time schedule when I get up in the morning and plot out the day. I make time for everything that has to be done, planning out the morning, afternoon and evening. Thus I keep all my affairs in order without any difficulty . . . In the evening before I go to bed, I review everything I have done that day . . . Better to lose sleep than time.[27]

This same spirit suffuses the Puritan ethic,[28] the maxims of Benjamin Franklin, and the conduct of the nineteenth-century burgher.

Closely associated with this attitude toward property is another trait characteristic of the bourgeois spirit: the importance attached to the *private sphere*. Quite apart from its content, which may be material or psychic, the private sphere is something sacred; any invasion into this sphere is a major offense. (The strong affective reactions against socialism, to be found even among many who have no property, can be explained in large measure by the fact that it represented a threat to the private sphere.)

What kind of relationships to others are characteristic for the "spirit" of bourgeois capitalism? The most striking is the limitation on sexual pleasure that was imposed by bourgeois sexual morality. Catholic morality is not in favor of such pleasure either, to be sure, but there is no doubt that *in practice* the conduct of the bourgeois-Protestant world was wholly different in this respect from that of the prebourgeois world. The feelings of a man like Benjamin Franklin reflect not only an ethical norm but also bourgeois practice. Under his treatment of the virtues, he has this to say about chastity (point 12): "Do not take pleasure in the delights of the flesh except for the sake of health or progeny. Never use them to the point of exhaustion or debilitation, or to the detriment of any one's peace and quiet."[29]

This devaluation of sexual pleasure corresponds to the reification of all human relationships within bourgeois society. Love relationships, in particular, were largely subordinated to economic considerations. Along with this re-

[27] Cited by Sombart, *op. cit.*, pp. 142–143.
[28] See Kraus, *op. cit.*, p. 259.
[29] Benjamin Franklin, *Autobiography*.

ification, an indifference to the fate of one's fellowman characterized relationships within the bourgeois world. This is not to say that there was no, or less cruelty in the pre-capitalist period. The point is that bourgeois indifference had its own distinctive nuance and tone: there was no trace of individual responsibility for the lot of others,[30] no hint of love for one's fellowmen as such without any conditions being attached.

Defoe provides us with a classic statement of this bourgeois indifference. He describes the poor "as a mob of whining ne'er-do-wells who are a disagreeable burden on the nation, requiring special laws."[31] As we know, capitalism actually operated with this outlook, particularly in the eighteenth and nineteenth centuries. Even as late as 1911, the American tobacco trust is accused of having the same attitude: "In the realm of competition, human beings were mercilessly pushed aside."[32] The lives of many nineteenth-century American industrial leaders provide ample illustrations.

In the bourgeois consciousness, this total lack of compassion did not seem unethical at all. On the contrary, it was anchored in certain religious or ethical conceptions. Instead of the blessedness guaranteed to those who were faithful children in the church; in the bourgeois concept, happiness was the reward for doing one's duty. And this idea was reinforced by the notion that in the capitalist system there was no limit to the success attainable by the competent individual.

This lack of compassion in the bourgeois character represented a necessary adaptation to the economic structure of the capitalist system. The principle of free competition, and the concomitant notion of the survival of the fittest, called for individuals who were not inhibited by compassion in their business dealings. Those who had the least compassion had the greatest chance of success.

Finally, we must mention another trait whose importance has been stressed by a wide variety of authors:

---

[30] Franklin lists these virtues as the most important ones: moderation, taciturnity, orderliness, resoluteness, thriftiness, diligence, sincerity, impartiality, temperance, cleanliness, imperturbability, chastity, and (later added!) humility. Characteristically enough, we find no mention of charity, love, and kindness.

[31] Daniel Defoe, *Giving Alms No Charity*, London, 1704, p. 426.

[32] Cited by Sombart, *op. cit.*, p. 234.

rationality, the principle of accounting and purposefulness. It seems to me that this bourgeois rationality, which has nothing to do with higher forms of reasoning activity, corresponds in large measure with the psychological notion of "orderliness" that we have described. Franklin's *Autobiography* provides typical examples of this peculiarly bourgeois "orderliness" and rationality.[33]

To sum up: as the chief traits of the bourgeois-capitalist spirit we have recognized: (1) restriction of the role of pleasure as an end in itself (particularly sexual pleasure); (2) retreat from love, with the emphasis instead on collecting, possessing, and saving as ends in themselves; (3) fulfillment of one's duty as the highest value; (4) emphasis on "orderliness" and exclusion of compassion for one's fellowman.

If we compare these character traits with the typical traits of the anal character described earlier, we can readily see that there seems to be a wide spectrum of agreement and correspondence. If this agreement is a fact, then we would be justified in saying that the typical libidinal structure of bourgeois man is characterized by an

[33] A fine example of this "orderliness" is Franklin's daily schedule, which he includes in his autobiography: The demands of order required that every portion of my activity have its proper time and place. So I drew up the following type of schedule for the entire day.

Early morning What good must I do today?	5) 6) 7)	Get up, wash, pray to the Godhead, plan my day and get to work, breakfast, etc.
	8) 9) 10) 11)	work
Noon	12)	read, go through my accounts, and eat lunch
Afternoon	1) 2) 3) 4) 5)	work
Evening What good have I done?	6) 7) 8) 9)	put things in order; eat supper; Music, relaxation, conversation; review the day.
Night	10) 11) 12) 1) 2) 3) 4)	sleep

Franklin also made up a list of his thirteen virtues, and checked off his offenses against them. This, too, embodies the same "orderliness" described by Abraham above.

intensification of the anal libido. A thorough study would provide a complete psychoanalytic description of bourgeois-capitalist character traits. It would also show how and to what extent these traits have developed as an adaptation to the requirements of the capitalist economic structure and to what extent, on the other hand, the underlying anal eroticism itself served as a productive force in the development of the capitalist economy.[84]

As I noted earlier, this paper does not deal with the question when to date the beginning of capitalism and the capitalist spirit. But to avoid some serious misunderstandings, we must give some consideration to development in monopolistic capitalism. It is clear that the typical character traits of the bourgeois of the nineteenth century gradually disappeared, as the classic type of the self-made, independent entrepreneur, who is both the owner and the manager of his own business, was disappearing. The character traits of the earlier business man became more of a handicap than a help to the new type of capitalist. A description and analysis of the latter's psyche in present-day capitalism is another task that should be undertaken by psychoanalytic social psychology.

In one social class, however, the earlier character traits persisted: i.e., among the lower middle class. In capitalistically advanced countries such as Germany, this class is economically and politically powerless; yet it continues to perform its economic task in the outmoded forms of an earlier (eighteenth- to nineteenth-century) capitalist epoch. In today's *petite bourgeoisie* we find the same anal character traits that have been ascribed to the older capitalist spirit.[85]

[84] I have stated earlier that it makes relatively little difference for the main thesis of this paper whether one speaks in terms of the libido theory or, as I have done in later years, in terms of energy-charged passions. At this point I want to mention that I have found the description of the anal character by Freud and others confirmed by the observable clinical data. My revision in *Man for Himself*, where the term "hoarding" is used instead of "anal" character, referred only to the *explanation* of the syndrome, which I see in a specific attitude toward others and things, rather than as being rooted in the anal erogenous zone. (It is true that feces and their equivalents play a special role in the hoarding character, but as symbolic expressions, rather than as "causes".) The term "hoarding character" could be used in this paper without changing the application to the spirit of capitalism. 1970.

[85] The analysis of the lower middle class is also an important task for social psychology. Particularly worthy of study is the revolutionary attitude peculiar to this class. It contains a mixture of rebellion and respect for paternal authority and discipline, which is characteristic of the anal

The working class seems to exhibit these anal character traits to a far lesser degree than the lower middle class.[36] This particular difference is easy enough to understand, when we consider that the worker's place in the process of production makes these traits obsolete.[37] The much more difficult question is this: Why do so many members of both the *proletariat* and the lower middle class, who have no capital, and no savings to speak of, still exhibit bourgeois-anal traits and the corresponding ideologies? The decisive reason, it seems to me, is that the libidinal structure underlying these traits is conditioned by the family and other traditional cultural factors. Thus it has a weight of its own, and it changes more slowly than the economic conditions to which it was adapted earlier.

What is the significance and importance of this kind of a social psychology for sociology? Its primary value lies in the fact that it enables us to understand the libidinal forces that find expression in character, in their role as factors which work to further (or inhibit) the social development of a society and its productive forces. It thus becomes possible to give a concrete, scientifically correct sense to the notion of the "spirit" of an epoch. If the notion of the "spirit" of a society is understood in these terms, it will make obsolete many of the controversies

---

attitude. The rebelliousness is not directed against the father's authority as such, which remains untouched despite everything. This ambivalent attitude is satisfied by splitting up the objects. The desire for authority is channeled toward the strong leader, while other specific father figures become the objects of rebellion.

The difference between the upper-class and lower-class bourgeoisie is clearly illustrated in the contrast between the anal jokes of the lower-class beer hall and the genital jokes of the upper-class wine cellar.

[36] Another important question is to what extent we can talk about an increase of genital character traits among the upper middle class. It is a difficult question to answer, precisely because the "genital character" has not been studied well enough in clinical and personal psychology.

[37] It should be clear that an analysis of the proletariat's character traits is very important for an understanding of the success and failure of socialism among this class. Here we shall merely note the contrast between the Marxian position (which places man's dignity and freedom above and beyond his economic activity, proclaims his unconditional right to happiness and satisfaction, and criticizes the reified character of human relationships within capitalism) and the anal traits of the bourgeois spirit which erroneously views Marxism as an attempt to demand an equal division of individual portions.

Closely related is another question, that we shall merely mention here. It concerns the retreat of paternal authority on the psychic level and the emergence of mother-centered traits. For example, the earth becomes a generous, giving mother for all her children. Related to this is the emancipation of women while the stress on masculine authority and the subjection of women is characteristic for lower middle class fascism. The relation of nationalism to the patriarchal structure of fascism also is part of this problematic area.

that are found in the sociological literature. For many of these controversies result from the fact that the notion of "spirit" refers to ideology, rather than to the character traits that can find expression in a wide variety of different and even opposing ideologies. The application of psychoanalysis will not only provide sociologists with useful viewpoints in their study of these questions; it will also prevent the uncritical use of false psychological categories.[38]

[38] The use of false and superficial psychological categories is typified by Sombart. He says of precapitalist man: "He is natural man, man as God created him . . . His economic attitude is clear to see, deriving from human nature itself" (Sombart, *op. cit.*, p. 11).

The same superficiality is found in his analysis of the psyche of the capitalist entrepreneur, which he claims is that of the child:

The ultimate values of such men represent a reduction of all psychic processes to their most simple elements . . . a regression to the simple state of the infantile psyche. Let me prove this. Four elementary value-complexes dominate the child's life: 1) physical size; 2) quick movement; 3) novelty; 4) the feeling of power. These same values, and only these I think, are also found in the value systems of modern man (Sombart, *op. cit.*, pp. 221 ff).

EPILOGUE

THIS BOOK HAS dealt with the crisis of psychoanalysis. Yet in order not to lose perspective it must be said that one cannot deal with this crisis without being aware that it is part of a larger one. Is it the crisis of contemporary society? Is it the crisis of man?

Yes, it is these, but the real crisis of today is one that is unique in human history: it is the *crisis of life itself*. Needless to repeat what those who know and care are trying to express as clearly as they can. We are confronted with the probability that within fifty years—and perhaps much sooner—life on this earth will have ceased to exist; not only because of nuclear, chemical and biological warfare (and every year technological progress makes weapons that are more devastating), but also because technological "progress" makes the soil, the water and the air unfit for the sustenance of life.

Has psychoanalysis any relevance in this crisis of life?

Perhaps not. Perhaps the dice have already been cast by the fact that both leaders and led, driven by their ambitions, greed, blindness and mental inertia, are so determined to proceed on the way to catastrophe that the minority, who see what is coming, are like the chorus of the Greek drama; they can comment on the tragic course, yet they lack the power to change it.

However, who can give up hope as long as there is life?

Who can be silent as long as there are billions of human beings, living, breathing, laughing, crying and hoping? The biologists, the chemists, the physiologists, the geneticists, the economists, the physicians, the theologians, the philosophers, the sociologists, the psychologists have spoken and are still speaking about the dangers; not the majority of them, but some; each from his particular field and point of observation. The psychoanalyst must speak from his point of observation. He knows, as do the others, that time is short and that he must stress the main issues.

At this point I can only stress what in my own way of thinking are the main issues; I have tried to indicate them in these papers, but after re-reading them I feel a summarizing statement to be in order. First of all, psychoanalysis deals with the issue of critical awareness, the uncovering of the deadly illusions and rationalizations that paralyze the power to act. Beyond this, I believe the most central issue to which psychoanalysis can make a contribution is the question of the attitude toward life itself. Here, however, psychoanalysis must part from Freud who, in the second part of his life believed that the craving for death and destruction is as fundamental and ineradicable a part of man as the striving for life. Others, like K. Lorenz, have claimed, although from a different theoretical standpoint, that man's aggressiveness is innate and can hardly be controlled.

In this enthusiasm to discover the innate character of destructiveness (which, incidentally, was quite convenient in rationalizing the inertia with regard to the danger of war), there has been almost no attempt to distinguish between entirely different kinds of aggressiveness: *reactive aggressiveness* in the service of life and as a defense against real—or alleged—threats to vital interests; *sadism*, the wish for omnipotence and complete control over human beings; *destructiveness*, the hate against life itself, and the wish to destroy it. Since one did not sufficiently differentiate between the various and completely different types of aggression, one could, of course, not even arrive at an attempt to study the conditions responsible for the presence and intensity of each of these forms of aggression, and much less the means to reduce their intensity.

The most fundamental problem, I believe, is the opposition between the love of life (biophilia) and the love of

death (necrophilia); not as two parallel biological tendencies, but as alternatives: biophilia as the biologically normal love of life, and necrophilia as its pathological perver-
sion, the love of and affinity to death.[1] Biophilia and
necrophilia often are found together in the same person;
what matters, whether blended or not, is the respective
intensity of these two fundamental passions. The majority
of people are not death lovers.[2] But they can be influenced, especially in times of crisis, by the desperate necro-
philes—and death lovers are always desperate. People can
fall under the influence of their slogans and ideologies
which, of course, hide and rationalize the real aim—that
of destruction. The death lovers speak in the name of
honor, order, property, the past—but sometimes also in the
name of the future, or freedom and justice. Psychoanalysis
teaches one to be skeptical of what a man *says*, because
his words usually reveal, at best, only his consciousness;
and to read between the lines, to listen with the "third
ear," to read his face, his gestures, and every expression of
his body.

Psychoanalysis can help people to spot the death lovers
behind their mask of lofty ideologies, and to see them for
what they are, and not for what they say. On the other
hand, to discover the life lovers, again not by their words,
but by their being. Above all it can help to discover the
necrophilious and biophilious elements in oneself; to see
this struggle, and to will the victory of one's own love of
life against its enemy. Speaking in the name of man, of
peace, or of God—these words remain ambiguous unless
they are accompanied by a word with which to begin and
to end: "In the name of Life!"

[1] Closely related to the malignant form of Freud's anal character.
[2] Preliminary studies by Michael Maccoby have shown that it is
reasonable to assume that extreme forms of necrophilia are to be found
in about 10 percent of various types of population in the United States
and in Mexico. Cf. Michael Maccoby, *Polling Emotional Attitudes in Relation to Political Choices.*